Dedication

To my buddy, Paul — after all the horse adventures, Packers games, and political discussions, we're still going strong.

To my parents, Gene and Lorraine — Dad, you gave me the love of learning and language. Mom, you gave me those things and the perseverance to get things done.

To my stepson, Paul — thanks for everything you do and who you are as a man.

Contents

Acknowledgments

I was a young kid growing up during the Green Bay Packers' glory years of the 1960s when I first heard the name "Johnny Blood" mentioned in my house. My parents seemed to recollect the person two different ways. My dad nodded in recognition of a superior football man. My mother smiled and said "Johnny Blood" in a strange "ooh-la-la" manner. It seemed like they were talking about a pirate or a movie star or a comic book hero, while I knew they were talking about an old-time player for the Packers. I was intrigued.

I was asked by my publisher to consider a biography on the great Don Hutson, which is well underway. But I suggested that a book on Johnny Blood was necessary first. I was unaware of any such effort to tell the John McNally story in full, though hundreds of articles had been written on the dashing Irishman. I wondered why that was. Why was Johnny Blood such an appealing subject for short articles, yet no one had attempted to fill in the gaps with a book?

Then I discovered what must be one of the most widely distributed unpublished books in history—*Vagabond Halfback: The Saga of Johnny Blood McNally* by Ralph Hickok. Hickok did a remarkable job of telling the full story, and he'd done it in the company of John himself. His manuscript was a joy to read, and his insights into the "vagabond halfback" were useful as I compared them with some of my original sources. However, I did not intend to tell the story as Ralph Hickok had. I couldn't, because I didn't have access to the subject. So, thank you Mr. Hickok.

In my own work on the Johnny Blood story, I proceeded to New Richmond, Wisconsin. You can't write a biography without walking the very same sidewalks as your subject. What I found in western Wisconsin was one of the most lovely, welcoming, and modern cities one could imagine. It was so great I took my daughter, Rachel, there with me twice because I knew the spirit of New Richmond and its citizens would have a positive impact on her character.

Therefore, I owe a debt of thanks to the gracious people I met in New Richmond, beginning with the wonderful Mary Zipperer, a distant cousin of John's. I'd found Mary's name in a newspaper article, called her out of the blue one day and told her what I was working on. And, from there, we were off. Mary made introductions and calls on my behalf. Together, we traveled to the McNally house. There, I met Steve Scott, who was restoring the house in which John McNally grew up and literally opened the doors to me. I was able to walk up the steps that John had crawled up more than once as both a young boy and a tipsy middle-aged man. I saw his room and imagined the joy he felt as a boy exploring that grand house and the surrounding neighborhood. I consider Mary a dear soul and a friend. Thanks, Mary.

From there, I encountered a host of gracious people in New Richmond, including the staffs at New Richmond High School and C. A. Friday Memorial Library, as well as Dave Newman at the *New Richmond News* and Mary Sather at the New Richmond Heritage Center. It was a pleasure to meet and speak with Tommy McNally, W. T. "Tom" Doar, Jr., Harold Lundell, Lyle Kellaher and his sons Len and Lee, Esther and Gerald Wentz, and Mary Beth Driscoll. Of supreme help was John Doar, a legend in his own right for his work in the U.S. civil rights movement, who knew and appreciated John McNally like few others.

The staffs of the Minneapolis Public Library, Minnesota Historical Society, and University of Minnesota also bear mention—especially Terry Stokke, who came through at the very last minute to help straighten out the story of how John McNally became Johnny Blood.

At St. John's University, archivist Brother David Klingermann OSB and Michael Hemmesh of the sports information department gave me wonderful assistance.

On the Green Bay end of things, Tom Murphy, archivist at the Packers Hall of Fame, must get a tip of the hat. He is a most-excellent gatekeeper to the heart of the legend that is the Green Bay Packers and a wonderful assistant to anyone doing work on team history. Mary Jane Herber, director of the Local History and Genealogy Department at the Brown County Library, also assisted me. Attorney C. J. "Joe" Stodola helped me with stories of John McNally in his coaching and teaching days at St. John's University. Lee Remmel, the inimitable Packers historian, also gave me several fascinating "Blood stories" to launch my pursuit.

Finally, thanks to my daughter, Rachel. Honey, you were the best eleven-year-old research assistant and copilot an author could find. Your help in New Richmond, Minneapolis, and at St. John's was immeasurable. And to think all I had to do to pay you back was spend four hours at the Mall of America! Of course, I had to laugh when we walked out of there and you said, "Dad, I think I have to take a bath. I was touched by a Vikings jersey." All joking aside, you are indeed my darling daughter. I am so proud of you.

Introduction

In an era that emphasized finding and playing your part in a growing United States, for reasons all their own, some men chose to buck the line. John Dillinger was one of these, a man whose father wanted nothing more for his son save settling down in a factory job or on a farm and raising a family. Dillinger couldn't do it. He began a life of crime in his teens and never looked back. He was the nation's first Public Enemy #1 and the familiar image on FBI firing range targets. By the time he was gunned down by that same FBI, just a few steps south of Chicago's Biograph Theater, he'd achieved something that the common soldiers of the assembly line and the plowed field would never have hazarded to dream. (But the rarefying countenance of that dream didn't escape their fancy either.) Curiously, Dillinger was heralded in his hometown as 'one helluva an athlete, a natural at second base.' There he was, at once accessible and still out of reach.

In a similar vein came a guy named John Victor McNally, who took a straighter path than Dillinger, though many a tongue wagged over his frequent departures from it. McNally's route to fame was football, something at which he was pretty damned good. He was the professional game's first superstar. By the time he and football parted ways in 1941, he'd etched his name deeply enough to be among the seventeen men named as charter members to pro football's hall of fame. His bust was put on permanent display there—safely away from the firing range.

This is a story about McNally, his prowess on the football gridiron and his amazing antics off it. But there's far more to this story than the exploits of one more talented and spoiled jock. Like all people who think outside the box, Blood spent much of his time, both sober and not, contemplating this life, this world, and his place in the mix. He was a genius in the truest sense of the word—possessing exceptional intellectual and creative power.

This is the story about a guy who, upon further and further review, made a conscious choice to be different. That choice didn't always play well with others. It didn't always play well with McNally. In explaining his relationship with his one-time coach, Curly Lambeau, he told a sportswriter, "Curly didn't completely understand me. But I don't perfectly understand myself." *That* coming from a poet, public speaker, merchant seaman, bartender, hotel desk clerk, war-time cryptographer, economics professor, and football star who must have understood himself at least as well as most. (Face it, he'd certainly met himself enough times, setting about his morning business, while the other part of him was just coming in from a night on the town.) Perhaps he didn't *perfectly* understand himself. That's why he spent eighty-two years partying and parlaying his way through the game, just trying to get familiar with who he was.

It was in the very early 1920s, that McNally grabbed the moniker "Blood" off a movie house marquee and made it his own. It was a little bit like sticking up a bank, a venial sin. He'd assumed the alias so he could skirt the NCAA rules about playing football for money while maintaining his college eligibility. No gun play, mind you, just a slight circumventing of the norm, a small disregard for what other people would think by a thrill-seeking kid. From there on, he was Johnny Blood, as derring-do a swashbuckler as Rudolph Valentino from whose movie he'd taken the name.

"Blood." What more did you have to say? "Dillinger" was good, but this was better—no dips or swerves in it. It was straightforward, with those half-hard consonants at the beginning and end and that semblance of "oooh" in the middle. A guy could play under just that one name, thereby inflating his self-constructed mystique. Then, if he got too far out of line and he needed to cover it up, he could toss "Johnny" out in front of it or drape the "McNally" over its backside.

But no matter how you said it, this wasn't John McNally, the bank president, or young Johnny McNally, the neighborhood hooligan. This was Blood—positioned somewhere in between the two and capable of either extreme, sometimes putting an arm around both of them in the very same instant. He had the heart of a daydreaming kid, the soul of a poet philosopher, and the mind of a scholar and a businessman.

There are those who suggest that John McNally never really came to terms with Johnny Blood—that the man himself sometimes got lost in the chasm between them—that he lost control over which side of that path he was walking on and, therefore, sometimes stumbled between them. But this was a clear example of Hegel's dialectic—a reconciliation between two opposite ideas ultimately resulting in positive forward impulsion—appreciable as a whole more than as opposing parts.

That the U.S. was changing as John McNally was aging is doubtless. In many ways, his story was the nation's story. McNally would grow up during the economic and global expansion between the turn of the century and the mid-teens, and hit his personal stride just after WWI. He'd live it up during the Roaring Twenties, cut it up during the Depression, and wander around seeking renewed adventure during WWII. In the 50s and 60s, he began cementing his legacy and, in the 70s, he'd coast into his twilight years while the young people of the nation were embracing his indigenous devil-may-care spirit. Born into the agrarian society of horse-and-buggy days, he'd bear witness to the advent of automobiles, radio, television, and computers. He'd see mankind walk on the moon and locate the *Titanic*, which had gone down in his youth. He died at the time Reagan and Gorbachev were about to tear down the wall. He'd seen everything change and everything—especially the matters of the human heart and soul—stay essentially the same.

Blood would have none of it and he'd have all of it. He embraced all that life had to offer while keeping its most mundane trappings at arms-length. He was a guy who was easy to talk about but difficult to describe—an enigma wrapped inside something perfectly understandable: the wish that all of us have to be completely free and confidently free-spirited. As an unabashed self-promoter, he was well ahead of the curve of today's entertainment industry icons. He was part rock star, part Hollywood idol and part Harry Houdini, his contemporary, all rolled into one. He eclipsed the antics of Terrell Owens and other such contemporary football personalities by some eighty years, though his motivation came from a far-less self-indulgent place in his psyche.

There are two ways to celebrate the life of Johnny Blood. One of them involves pushing the envelope until dawn or later, bending what some might see as legal, moral, and health-conscious imperatives. The other lies in being as totally true to ourselves as we can muster, and then playing the game for all it's worth. Either way, it means coming out the better for it—as long as we maintain what his good friend John Doar called "balance." Here's a good old Irish toast, with or without distilled spirits, to one John "Johnny Blood" McNally, who clearly was cut from a kind of cloth they don't seem to make much anymore.

Chapter 1

Growing up in "Nouveau-Riche-mond" (1903–1919)

In all my years before, I never knew
A morn so full of leaping, pulsing joy.
I bound, barefoot, o'er the grass refreshed with rain,
Such quickening draughts 'ere this I never drew,
Of pleasure deep as life, and sharp as pain.
Dear God! How sweet in spring it is to be a boy!

— John V. McNally

It was John McNally himself who, when returning to New Richmond, Wisconsin, with author Ralph Hickok, seemed to dismiss his boyhood town by tagging it "Nouveau-Riche-mond." But that made some sense. McNally's relationship with his hometown had always flickered—sometimes characterized by a warm embrace and a hardy pat on the back, sometimes by a cold stare, a wagging tongue, and a self-righteous whisper.

That relationship hadn't been a typical one, even when John was a boy. Of course, he wasn't a typical boy. In a sense, he'd *blazed* through New Richmond, rather than grown up there.

Today, New Richmond remains a quaint little city handily tucked north of a bustling interstate highway, an easy half-hour drive from Minneapolis–St. Paul. New Richmond calls itself "The City Beautiful," and no serious remonstration has ever arisen to deny its claim. It's a welcoming, small town that balances progress and history along with urbanization and rural charm. It has the fifth-busiest airport in Wisconsin, boasting 47,000 flights in and out a year.

New Richmond's calendar of events says much about its character. Its strong Irish tradition is acknowledged with a St. Patrick's Day parade, and its homespun values and history are celebrated with Good Neighbor Days, the New Richmond Fun Fest, St. Croix County Farm–City Days, and Heritage Days.

Kids still fish from the railroad bridge, the streets are clean and wide, and the parks bustle with activity. The holidays are still celebrated in small-town tradition with community members gathering at schools and churches for traditional holiday fare.

Not very far out of town are the remnants and revisions of once-thriving farmland punctuated by steep hills and winding river ravines. Trees great and small have cropped up in these places. The topography is a combination of prairie, wetlands, ponds, and lakes. The waterways offer recreational opportunities that have become a part of the area's tourist economy. Over his lifetime, John McNally came to know this terrain well, exploring every nook and cranny of it ("as something of a geography buff" said his long-time friend John Doar) in search of his own roots.

As the result of a June 12, 1899, cyclone that took seven minutes to wipe out much of a previous half century of progress, New Richmond is also hailed as "The City That Built Itself Twice." The town of 6,800 embraces that piece of history because it says much about its work ethic. It is claimed that by the end of the cyclone year, New Richmond's business district was up and running again.

Nearly lost in the cyclone's rubble, according to one legend, was a young lawyer—Bill McNally, John McNally's grandfather, who'd been at work in his downtown office when the twister hit. As his rescuers searched the ruins, they expected to find the body of a loved one. Instead, they found a survivor. Digging out from a pile of trouble would prove a necessary family trait handed down over the generations—a gift, as it were, from grandfather to grandson.

That New Richmond still touts the neighborliness of a bygone era is evident in its invitation to visitors to take a walking tour of its West First

Street Historic District. These are well-tended private homes, set just west of the downtown business district, reflective of a time when a town's merchants and professional men walked from their homes to their places of business on Main Street (now Knowles Avenue). The tour boasts some 25 buildings on the National Register of Historic Places. Resplendent examples of Italian, Colonial Revival, Arts and Crafts, Eastlake, Queen Anne, and even "Steamboat Gothic" architecture are represented in these homes.

"New Richmond Must Be Rebuilt" read the headline of the *St. Croix Republican* on June 15, 1899. Three days earlier a cyclone had erased much of downtown New Richmond. By the time of this picture, the "new" New Richmond had gotten miraculously to its feet, as this shot of Main Street attests. Photograph obtained from and used with the permission of the New Richmond Heritage Center.

It was into this neighborhood, and into one of its well-known and prosperous families, that John Victor McNally, Jr., was born on November 27, 1903. The McNally home, of Queen Anne styling, still sits strikingly on the southeast corner of West Second Street and Montana Avenue. Built in 1894, the house was originally the home of Erick J. Thompson. Prior to the 1899 cyclone, Thompson had been a successful clothier in New Richmond. Like most of the homes in this well-heeled part of the city, Thompson's house was spared by the cyclone. But Thompson decided not to rebuild his own downtown business, and in 1900 he sold his home to John McNally, Sr., for $3,500.

McNally had married Mary Celestina Murphy in 1898. He was 32, and she was 20. It was probably a step in the right direction for him. For her, it was more likely a project in taking the rough edges off a man raised near the lusty crossroads town just east of New Richmond called Erin Prairie or Erin Corners. In 1929, John, Jr., wrote of his parents' commingling in this way:

> Erin [Prairie] became the center of considerable roughhouse activity which continued until the logging was exhausted. Erin once had nine saloons, a black smith shop, a hotel, a church and two grocery stores. It teemed with liquor, talk, fighting, laughter and bragging. From this environment came the McNally's. The Murphy's in Hammond were in a slightly more refined community. They were on the railroad and in close contact with the world outside. There the formalities and amenities met more observance. But it could not be said to be highly polished.

By 1900, Mary had ended her teaching career of two years, and McNally was well entrenched as the manager of the New Richmond Roller Mills. His brothers, Miles and William, owned the mill and served as its attorneys. William had married Mary Murphy's sister.

At age 26, John, Jr., described his father as follows:

> He was 5'11" and 170 pounds. He was quick, athletic, vigorous, powerful, elastic and vital. His temperament was gay and volatile. He was left-handed, black haired, hazel eyed and very witty—a clever mimic and keen raconteur. His sense of humor was widely known and his laugh was pleasing, quick and contagious. His eyes were large and sparkling.

His description of his mother went like this:

> She was 5'8" and about 119 pounds, hazel eyes, and brown hair, with fair complexion. Her favorite sport was breaking colts to ride. She had a reputation for great physical courage. She was educated in rural schools and at River Falls Teachers College.

Irish heritage surged through the McNally veins as well as the household. Sitting one generation back were the clans Murphy, McGraw, McNally, and McCormick. Back another rung they were joined by McGuff, McGannon,

Riley, and Barrett. The Irish potato famine and a stifling feudalism had driven nearly one fourth of the Irish population to America by 1860. Thanks to its farming opportunities and its topographic similarities to Ireland, Wisconsin became a natural place to settle. Work on the railroad and in the lumbering industry offered Irish laborers opportunity, as well.

The massive McNally home at 350 West Second Street sat far enough away from the streets to accentuate its beauty and provide an expansive lawn on which the McNally children would play—and McNally children there would be.

John was the fourth of six surviving children born to the McNallys in this home. John and Mary's first child died at or shortly after birth, in June 1900. Then came three girls, Lucille, Helen, and Honor. The birth of John, Jr., on Thanksgiving Day, was cause for a father's joy and little time was wasted in bestowing the father's name on this first son. In 1908, another son, James, was born and died. Three years later, James M. was born, presenting John with a younger brother to both torment and drag around town as a mascot. Then, in 1915, Margaret was born to round out the family.

John and Mary McNally's family included sisters (in birth order) Lucille, Helen, and Honor. Then came John Jr., James M., and Margaret. Photograph obtained from and used with the permission of John Doar.

The verve and synergy between his parents' disparate personalities both confused John and made him who he was. On one hand was his mother, as sophisticated and cultured a woman as could rise up from the hilly farmland northwest of tiny Hammond, Wisconsin. On the other hand was his father, a rambunctious entertainer borne out of Erin Prairie who embraced life with a robustness that drew others to him. Both were highly intelligent—but John's mother continuously refined her intelligence through literature and music and contemplation, while his father parlayed his intelligence to reconnoiter his way through the world.

It was in the grand living room of the McNally house that a three- or four-year-old John would find himself standing between his parents who had positioned themselves opposite one another. "Which one do you love the most, Johnny?" his doting parents would both ask, cajoling him to pick one of them. "Come to the one you love the most." John would stand between them, recalled his Aunt Margaret, paralyzed, looking back and forth at the two of them. It was also Aunt Margaret who suggested they stop the game, stating, "You're tearing that poor boy in half."

It's tempting to speculate on the role this kind of incident may have played in fostering the many complexities and conflicts that were to beset McNally as an adult. Though he told Ralph Hickok he had no personal recollection of the event, John also asked him not to publish the biography he went on to write, most likely, Hickok believed, because he'd included this story in it. By today's standards the anecdote is barely noteworthy. But perhaps the story touched a bit too closely on what John saw as some subconscious, irreconcilable aspects of his own personality for him to be comfortable with it in print.

The huge elm and maple trees in the yard provided plenty of limbs for climbing and shade on hot summer days. Behind the house, sloping down to Third Street, was a half block of veritable wilderness made up of trees, undergrowth, and even a small pond. It contrasted with and yet flowed from the well-manicured yard. It was ripe for exploration, and John's readiness for adventure was born on forays in the backyard.

It was from this massive, wonderful white house that all the McNally kids would venture in their various ways. Lucille would marry, have a child, and end up in Maine. Helen would get a degree from the University of Minnesota and return to teach history for many years at New Richmond High School. She would remain single her entire life. Honor

John Jr. with parents John Sr. and Mary. Photograph obtained from and used with the permission of John Doar.

would marry, move to New York, raise three children, die in Florida, and be buried in New Richmond. "Jim" would also remain in New Richmond all his life and never marry. Margaret would marry, raise three children, and also end up in Maine. In later years, Helen and Jim lived in the family house on West Second Street, and John lived with them for stretches of time as a semi-permanent resident and as a guest when he resided elsewhere. He had a permanent bedroom on the second floor.

As they ventured out, the McNally kids, children of some affluence, took with them a distinct attitude and a certain permission to be different. They could get away with it. One former neighbor described the McNally kids—especially the three that remained associated with New Richmond in later years—as "universally talented and smart, though a little quirky."

The grand McNally home still stands on the southeast corner of West Second Street and Montana Avenue in New Richmond, Wisconsin—"The City Beautiful." Photograph obtained from and used with the permission of W. T. "Tom" Doar, Jr.

That is not to say they were aloof or snobbish. Helen was a respected—even revered—teacher at the high school, and John returned to town as a popular prodigal son on many occasions, despite his foibles. Many described Jim as the most distant and flaky of the lot, especially in later years, citing strolls downtown in his pajamas as supporting evidence.

"John came from the rich part of town," said Harold Lundell, who grew up several years John's junior, "but he spent time on the north side. His family didn't think they were better than other people. They were down to earth."

"Every one of them was very intelligent," remembered neighbor Esther Wentz, "but they each had their idiosyncrasies."

The joys of youth in the grand McNally house represented freedom and exploration. John suggested that, as a kid, he was "small" and "precocious." He said he was "too small to participate in any kind of athletics. Unless you count climbing. I loved to climb things. Trees, telephone poles, the outside of houses." John's love of climbing would manifest itself in various ways over the years, including an adventure at age four that would excite and terrify any toddler. He climbed out his bedroom window and up an eave trough to the peak of the three-story house. There he sat until his father came home from work and got a ladder out to take him down. "I still don't know why I did something like that," he told Hickok. He added,

> I suppose no one knows why he did things when he was four. But there have been so many things, so much like that, since I've been old enough to know better, that are just as hard for me to explain. I suppose I must have a strong need for attention. I can't explain some of the things I've done on any other basis.

John also remembered for author Richard Whittingham playing "an old child's game" called "Run, Run, Forward." In the game, he recalled, "there was a lot of tackling, that sort of thing. This was around 1910. I was very young when I got into it." John described himself as a kid "who was full of run." He told Hickok that he "loved to get out and run and jump and climb trees in the fields and in the jungle" near the Willow River. Eventually, climbing and running would be common themes in some of the wildest stories from his days as a Green Bay Packer.

John's early adventures around and *on* the house were just a start, of course. The Willow River lay a couple of blocks to the north and west, and a slightly older John was known to venture in that direction, as well. One swimming hole in town was located in the "widespread" on the east side of Main Street a bit past the present-day beach at what is now Mary Park. The "widespread" was a term in town for the area of the Willow that opened up into what appeared to be a lake. John spent many summer hours there in the company of neighborhood friends.

He told Whittingham,

> Starting when I was in kindergarten, I went around with boys who were always two or three years older than I was, played with them and tried to compete in their games. I wasn't as physically developed as they were and consequently got knocked around a lot. No one ever considered that I would wind up being an athlete back then.

But the widespread wasn't the most popular place to swim in town. A couple of blocks west, the Willow flowed under Main Street as it made its way to Hudson, the St. Croix County seat, and then the Mississippi River. New Richmond kids had always used the area around the bridge as a swimming hole, often diving from the bridge proper at road level. But inevitably a few brave souls would scale the bridge girders to the very top and dive into the Willow River about twenty-five feet below.

And so it was that a twelve-year-old John McNally found himself with his feet on that top girder and the Willow wending its way under the bridge far beneath him. Fear gripped him; he was in the throes of another dilemma. He could dive as promised or climb back down in disgrace.

He'd climbed up to the top of the bridge on a friend's dare, he told Hickok. "It was kind of a tradition that a couple of kids would do that on the Fourth of July. I didn't plan to be one of them … I was scared to death. I didn't want to jump. But, with all those people watching, I had to. So I did." It was his first public display of derring-do. It would hardly be his last. It was the type of performance he would replicate often as a professional football player, particularly with the Packers. But by then, he had become adjusted to the notoriety.

Another of John's exercises in climbing involved the dangerous practice of jumping on and off moving trains. With a dozen or so trains coming through town each day, he had lots of opportunities to practice. "We used to hop on the freight cars here," he told Hickok from near the old swimming hole, "ride the three blocks, and then hop off again. It was a pretty good training ground."

Other times, John and friends would catch a train all the way to Hudson, some fifteen miles to the southwest, and then catch another one back home. "It was part of growing up in a small town in Wisconsin back then," he told Whittingham. "Hitching rides on these trains was a sport to all of us."

He told Hickok of the time when his father caught him on one of his three-block jaunts and the ensuing thrashing he received. "It was the worst whipping I ever got. I had marks for weeks," he said.

There were also some occasions when John would ride the train a good distance in the engine with a friendly engineer, but those trips were sanctioned affairs done with the blessing of his parents and the train operators. They weren't nearly as much fun.

John's love of trains would be another thread from his early days that would weave its way into the lore of his time as a Packer. He explained its source to Whittingham:

> Freight trains and passenger trains, that was the way you moved most things in those days. And I would hear this lon-n-n-g whistle, very plaintive and compelling; it was very romantic to a child. Far away places, dreams, new worlds, all that kind of thing.

It was near the train depot that young John got his first close-up glimpse of a different kind of life—hoboes. The thick undergrowth along the river and near the depot formed something of a jungle, McNally told Hickok. "The hoboes would come in from all directions, and this jungle area here was their hangout. We had them by the scores."

Farm life was a passing part of young McNally's experience. As a youngster, he would join other kids on the Fay farm where they made some money by picking fruits and vegetables. When he was a little older, he spent summers on the Murphy farm outside of Hammond, helping put up hay. His grandparents' farm was described as "well kept"—suggesting that diligence and hard work was the norm there. John wasn't reported to embrace farm life, especially its physical demands.

Even though it was never openly conveyed to him, John grew up believing that his slight frame was something of a disappointment to his father. Athletics had been a strong theme in the McNally family. John, Sr., was an avid boxing fan and a proponent of America's pastime—baseball.

At least two photos exist of young John in baseball uniforms taken at the McNally house. The first is of a five- or six-year-old bedecked in the moleskin baseball pants and heavy shirt of the time. He has a catcher's glove on his right hand and, with a slight grin on his face, appears ready to catch a ball from his dad.

The second picture, from 1911, is of seven-year-old John, Jr., along with his father and three other people: W. T. Doar, Sr.; Paul McNally, John's thirteen-year-old cousin; and a New Richmond dentist, Dr. Sherman. John's uniform, emblazoned with the word "Minneapolis," came from his uncle, Mike Cantillon, who was the owner of the Minneapolis Millers. Taken on the southeast part of the yard near the corner of the large front porch, the

John in the canvas baseball outfit of the day alongside the McNally home, waiting to catch a lobbed pitch from his dad. Photograph obtained from and used with the permission of John Doar.

shot shows the elder McNally in a joyous pose, as though he were about to haul in the fly ball to end the World Series. John told Hickok that his dad was "always happy to box with me, or to get me out on the lawn, and pitch to me, or bat the ball to me." The senior McNally also filled out the infield on a New Richmond town team with three of his brothers.

Doar's presence in the photograph is noteworthy. The relationship between the Doars and the McNallys dates back to 1908 when Doar, an aspiring young attorney, moved to New Richmond. His second cousin was Mary McNally, and she suggested that W. T. share John's upstairs bedroom until he found a place of his own. He ended up staying with the McNallys for five years, until he married and his law practice was well established.

Members of the extended McNally family were also athletic. Years later, after John had achieved fame as a football player, he would often take a picture of the 1915 New Richmond High School championship baseball team off the wall of Kellaher's Bar and point out his cousins, saying, "I wasn't the only athlete in the family."

John's sisters, Honor and Helen, had also taken to basketball in a big way, helping their high school team to back-to-back undefeated seasons. It was said that they could throw baseballs (and snowballs) as well as any boy in their neighborhood. It was even rumored that when Helen went to the University of Minnesota, she was asked not to go out for basketball because she was so dominating that her side always won and it was no fun for the other players.

Thanks to its proximity to Immaculate Conception Catholic Church, the McNally home became a gathering place to a large contingency of McNallys after Sunday mass. Summer brought cousins chasing around the house and yard, while winter meant large gatherings filled with holiday cheer. At the center of these gatherings was the senior McNally, who could tell jokes and stories as well as he could toss a cousin into the air. Mary was always there to keep a lid on all the activity and to converse about the goings-on in New Richmond and the world at large.

"America's Pastime." W. T. Doar, Paul McNally, John McNally, Jr., Dr. Sherman, and John McNally, Sr. The elder McNally is ebullient—for the game, the day, the spring. Photograph obtained from and used with the permission of the C. A. Friday Memorial Library.

The entire age was one of change and expansion, and the McNally house and its occupants seemed to be totally in synch with the world around them and, as a result, very modern. In the Roosevelt era, social life, entertainment, outdoor recreation, and technology all saw major change. By 1910, progressive reforms were also improving the lives of citizens. The McNallys were emblematic of the general enthusiasm of the era. In 1901, Theodore Roosevelt assumed the presidency following the assassination of William McKinley. At 42, Roosevelt was the youngest man ever to lead the nation. It was the Age of Optimism, thanks in large part to Roosevelt's own panache. Once described as a "steam engine in trousers," Roosevelt shrugged off the mantle of aristocracy to become a man of the people. He was an avid learner and a devotee of "the strenuous life." Over his life, he would write twenty-four books and his interests ran from mammals and birds to warfare and art history.

Roosevelt, the rough-riding outdoorsman, had a very clear impact on the sports world, as well. Baseball had already enjoyed a good run as America's pastime, but football was now beginning to grow in popularity, despite its brutal nature and annual death toll. In 1905, Roosevelt's own son would be seriously injured on the gridiron, and Roosevelt's hand on the sport would help produce the National Collegiate Athletic Association.

With all its growth and change, the first decade of the 1900s made the country seem as though it were in constant motion. "Life in the States is one perpetual whirl of telephones, phonographs, electric bells, motors, lifts, and automatic instruments," noted a visiting Englishman. So was New Richmond. And so was the McNally household.

John's upbringing wasn't all about athletic feats or the lack thereof. And it should be noted that, thus far, John's athletic feats had all been of the solitary variety, as he was too small for any kind of team sports. But with Mary McNally as his mother, John was also going to have to earn some laurels from the cultural and academic side of life. And, he did. In fact, his first-grade teacher, Mrs. W. T. Doar, often described young John McNally as "far and away the smartest student" she'd ever taught.

At age eight, John recited Rudyard Kipling's "Gunga Din" in a public performance at Hagan's Opera House on Main Street in downtown New Richmond. John had been put up to the performance in a confab between his mother and Mrs. Doar, his teacher. Following the performance, he was hailed by many in New Richmond as a gifted boy. John had trained for a presentation like this since before he could read.

An eight-year-old John McNally recited Rudyard Kipling's "Gunga Din" one night at Hagan's Opera House on Main Street in New Richmond. Photograph obtained from and used with the permission of John Doar.

His mother had seen to it that the boy had an early introduction to Greek, Roman, and Irish mythology. She also had him memorize and recite great blocks of poetry. Two absolutes in this regard were Shakespeare and Kipling. Public performance such as that at Hagan's were a natural outcropping of his mother's penchant for learning and his father's penchant for performance. It was really the start of a great career in public performance—as likely to take place on the gridiron as it was the street corner, much of it with Kipling as a touchstone.

As the byproduct of the Murphy–McNally partnership formed in the Roosevelt era, young John was going to have a relationship with the world characterized by more than just outward flamboyance. He would also possess a curiosity about things around him. It would be the classic one–two punch. Learning and teaching. Studying and performing. Thinking outside the box in order to understand the box. In his adventures, John had done more than climb trees or houses or trains, he'd asked questions. There's little doubt that growing up in a family of means offered him a certain luxury to do this rather than concern himself with the constant grubbing necessitated by a poorer existence.

But John's curiosity, the lessons of his father's stage presence and need to perform and his mother's more sedate and studious approach, would combine to make him an outstanding student. His parents' freethinking ways taught him that education was not dependent on going to school. At an early age, and quite removed from any homework assignment or classroom, John's mother had him memorizing and reciting the classics, and studying public speaking and debate. He also took violin lessons.

It wasn't all a success, either. He told Hickok of a particularly embarrassing crash he experienced at a tortured violin recital at age 12 or 13. The random notes of the song he played seemed to have little in common with "Turkey in the Straw." He left the stage, humiliated. "I haven't gotten over it yet," he said as a man of nearly seventy.

At St. John's University a few years later, John's first contribution to the school newspaper would be called "Failure as a By-Product." In it, he wrote, "Nothing seems to contribute so much to the ultimate success of a man as a few real failures, nor anything to be so fatal to a budding career as an easy initial success."

John found his way through elementary school with great success, switching back and forth between the Catholic school just two blocks from his house and the public school several blocks south and east, across Main Street. His mother had doubts about the worldliness of a completely Catholic education, something on which she and the parish priest would clash.

John McNally scooted through the New Richmond High School curriculum, graduating at age fourteen. He put in another year "studying typing and commercial subjects" in what he called "graduate high school." Photograph obtained from and used with the permission of the New Richmond Heritage Center.

John relayed to Ralph Hickok a series of calamitous events that followed this clash, which may make one ponder earthly matters and the after life. John described his mother as a "free-thinking Catholic." Obviously, the description didn't fit the priest. One Sunday, following John's transfer back to the public school, the parish priest gave a sermon scolding parishioners who deprived their children of a good Catholic education. Mary McNally was pretty sure the lecture was pointed in her direction and she demonstrably led the family out of church. A few days later, John's dad saw the priest on the sidewalk near the McNally home and gave him a piece of his own mind. He told the priest if he ever did anything like that again, he'd "rip off his clerical collar and beat the daylights out of him." The next day, the priest was dead—a victim of a car-train accident.

Wherever John attended school, he mastered the material and impressed his teachers He was one of those students who made it all look so easy. He was already an accomplished learner when he came to school. Mary had seen to it. In addition to Mrs. Doar, his other teachers gave him high marks along with high expectations. Was it any surprise, then, that John graduated from high school by age fourteen, having finished off the curriculum at New Richmond High School? In a motivated McNally household, regular schooling was a mere formality, having little to do with actual education.

In his high school graduation picture, John is seated front and center, surrounded by his older classmates at the high school entrance. Across the bottom is written "Class of 1918. New Richmond High School." John is much smaller than his classmates, and he is wearing short pants. He seems more "mascot" than "peer." Yet he's done in two years what they've done in four. He is a part of the group and, yet, beyond it.

John sat front and center in his high school graduation photograph because he was clearly different from his fellow graduates. He'd done in two years what they'd done in four. He was, said Mrs. Doar, his first-grade teacher, "far and away the smartest student" she'd ever taught. Photograph obtained from and used with the permission of John Doar.

The following autumn, he returned part-time to the high school to study "typing and commercial subjects." His parents felt he was too young to start college. During this year, which he referred to as "graduate-high school," he also did a lot of reading. He remembered:

> It was in those days I first read about Cincinnatus, the Roman general who would farm his land until war came, then would lead his troops to victory and go back to farming again. I made him my hero and, as I grew older, I realized that what Cincinnatus was, was a clutch hitter. I'm a great admirer of clutch hitters.

It was almost time for John to leave his boyhood home and his childhood behind. He would return to New Richmond again and again over the rest of his life, but the understandings between John, the townsfolk, and his family would never be predictable. At times, the citizens of New Richmond would seem more appreciative of the vagabond halfback than his own family. At other times, the McNally home and family would be the only safe harbor away from the storms of a nomadic life. He always held "a real affection for his roots," said long-time friend John Doar. But he also often felt a shroud of disappointment awaiting him, especially from his own family, because he'd put his shoulder into professional football rather than the many respectable opportunities afforded him.

On November 27, a precocious John turned fifteen. Another Thanksgiving and Christmas would pass, then another St. Patrick's Day and Easter. Summer would come and go. That fall, he would be off to his mother's alma mater, River Falls Normal School, about twenty miles due south.

So far, he had done very little to determine whether he, himself, was a clutch hitter. He'd really had very few chances to test his mettle in that regard. He'd gotten off the roof with his dad's help, and he'd made it on and off the trains by himself all right. He'd jumped from the bridge into the Willow River with the eyes of a crowd pushing him. He'd mastered the academic challenges sent his way, though they had actually come rather easily.

The jury was still out on his ability to pull it together under pressure, to maintain his confidence in the face of chaos. He was heading off with a box of untested tools. His upbringing, marked by as much culture and wealth as might be hoped for in a small Wisconsin town, may well have proved to be his undoing. Sure, it had given him a certain stroll, but had it prepared him for the tough times? He was just fifteen, nearly sixteen, and he was headed out of town, this time on a train from which he wasn't supposed to jump.

Within five years, he would find some balance, hit his athletic stride, assume his stage presence under the moniker "Johnny Blood," and become one of the greatest clutch hitters to ever play the game of football and, perhaps, life. He would indeed be "a boy in spring." But not before he'd experienced a few failures.

Chapter 2

A Boy in Spring Sees the Stars
(1919–1923)

What aureole beauty ascends in the night
When Northern Aurora shimmers soft, glowing light;
Darting and crossing, here, thither, and yon,
Hardly we follow it, ere it is gone.

— John V. McNally

If John had found wanderlust while kicking around his hometown of New Richmond, it was just beginning to be realized as he headed south in the fall of 1919 to begin his college career in River Falls. He was a boy in spring all right, and the world was his oyster, steamed open and there for the tasting. He'd left New Richmond confident and somewhat self-satisfied. He'd conquered the classrooms and the textbooks there and acquired a nascent athleticism. He was feeling the power and the joy of youth. Could he control it?

About 225 miles due east of New Richmond sits Green Bay, Wisconsin. On the night of August 11, 1919, just as John was putting the finishing touches on the last summer of his youth, a meeting was held to organize a town team to play football that fall. Thanks to the sponsorship of a Green Bay meat-packing company, this team would become forever known as the "Packers." Eventually, John's meandering would take him to Green Bay for the first time, as a Packer player. Then, he'd return again and again over the years. Though John didn't know it that August evening, a piece of his destiny was being prepared for him.

As colleges went, River Falls was a practical place, designed primarily to turn out teachers to fill Wisconsin's many rural schools. The Normal School wasn't frilly; it wasn't meant to be. It consisted of an old, staid brick building that housed the classrooms and the theater as well as the gymnasium. Not that the gymnasium captured John's interest—he still hadn't developed a serious bent for athletic pursuits. However, thanks to another interest that would occupy him for much of the rest of his life, he was about to suspend, for a time, his pursuit of serious study.

John's time at River Falls, he told Ralph Hickok, was basically about "Puberty. Adolescence. I was discovering girls, I had temporarily lost interest in books, I was away from home and feeling my oats. In River Falls, I behaved differently than I ever had in New Richmond." On November 27, he turned sixteen. Now on his own, his youthful achievements came tumbling down around his ankles. He wasn't close to ready for the independence of college life.

John told Hickok he'd learned a little trick at the school that could assist him in his hanky-panky. Near a fire escape on one of the buildings at River Falls, he would "put something in the door to keep it open. Then, that night, I'd bring a girl up the fire escape, through the door and onto the stage for a little romancing." John's preoccupation with romancing proved to be part of his problem and the resulting performances on stage were nothing that his parents had encouraged.

John's brother, Jim, told Hickok of another occasion involving a girl and the McNally house, which was vacant that winter with Jim staying at his Uncle Will's house:

> I used to come back to the house to play in the yard sometimes, and one day I saw John bring this girl—I'll call her Mary Jones—into the house. He had a key. Well, I didn't say anything then. But later, our parents were going to come back, I saw him at the house again, on the front porch. Well, you know how little brothers are—I went up to him and said, 'I saw you bring Mary Jones into the house one day.'

John kept insisting that Jim tell him why he thought John had brought "Mary" into the house. Finally, Jim suggested that John had brought her in there to have sex with her. "So John grabbed an axe that we had out there on the front porch," Jim told Hickok.

> And he put my head over the railing, and he said he'd cut it off if I didn't promise not to tell. I didn't think he would, at first, but he kept holding me there, and I got scared and began to think maybe he would cut it off, so I promised not to tell. I guess he felt bad then, seeing how scared I was, because he gave me the axe and put his head on the railing and said, 'Now I'm going to let you cut my head off.' But, of course, I couldn't do that.

Although sex had definitely drawn John's attention from his studies, his efforts at River Falls were further hampered when his parents left for California for the winter, leaving John with a checkbook. It would prove to be a winter of excess—sexually and financially—followed by one serious hangover of regret. By spring, John wasn't feeling so joyous. His parents were on their way back, the checkbook had become an albatross and, for the first time in his life, he hadn't been up to the challenges of school. His grades at River Falls were nothing to stem the tide of disappointment that was coming his way.

John decided to head off to sea ahead of the storm of his parents' return, a scheme he'd no doubt picked up when reading *Moby Dick*. Thanks to a savvy Navy recruiter, however, his plans for a life of redemption at sea were cut short. The recruiter knew John was too young for the service. But rather than squabble, he simply told John his vision wasn't up to snuff. John's Ishmaelian plans were nixed. Instead, he climbed onto a freight train and headed for South Dakota where his uncle, Fred Murphy, owned a farm. John had never loved farm work, but now, fully immersed in it, he realized just how much he hated it.

By the time summer had started in earnest, he was headed back by rail to New Richmond. He'd go to work for Uncle Fred once more, this time at the *Minneapolis Tribune*, which Fred Murphy later would publish. It was John's first trip back to New Richmond to reclaim some of his faded glory, but not his last. He would pass the rest of the summer somewhat in the mode of his former carefree youth before heading off to Collegeville,

Minnesota, to continue his academic career. This time, it would be his father's alma mater—St. John's University, the oldest Catholic university in the northwestern United States.

John's arrival in Collegeville at the end of summer in 1920 was less than spectacular. After all, he was just another new face on campus and he was coming off a couple of bumps in the road, his abject performance at River Falls and the abuse of his parents' trust. But his arrival at St. John's would mark the beginning of a relationship that would endure, on and off, for some sixty years. His first walk across the campus must have put all of his previous success and failure into perspective. Here in remote central Minnesota, he'd be able to focus—without girls and without a checkbook.

Tom Roeser, a former St. John's student and reporter for the *Minnesota Daily Times*, St. Cloud, recorded McNally's acclimation to St. John's that autumn:

> The first day McNally spent at St. John's he attended classes and spent the afternoon walking around the campus swinging a stick he had found in the woods. By suppertime he had many friends. He liked people as they liked him, but he could do without them. He loved to walk and throw pebbles, throw them as far as he could. He loved to jump hedges. He would walk down the corridors, leap suddenly, and touch each chandelier. After he had passed, a corridor-full of chandeliers were swinging perilously.
>
> He walked a lot the first fall. Then he began to take an interest in running. McNally, it developed, had lightning speed and long wind.

One can duplicate John McNally's travels across the campus of St. John's today and understand why he took to the place as much as he did—especially if one has just left New Richmond. Progress has not stood still since McNally graced the place, however. Campus architecture is surprisingly modern. Marcel Breuer and Associates of New York designed a dominating sculpture called "The Banner of the Cross," the large church behind it, and the campus library. Breuer, of the Bauhaus school, also laid out a 100-year plan for the university's ongoing development.

Despite the modern buildings and steady progress, the stately quality

This is a 1914 game at St. John's. By the 1920s, baseball was being slowly eclipsed in popularity by rough-neck gridiron action. Photograph obtained from and used with the permission of St. John's University.

of the campus remains solidly intact. One realizes that St. John's holds much of the same intrinsic balance of progress and history, of the pastoral and urbane, found in "The City Beautiful." Along one edge of the campus sits lovely Lake Sagatagan in place of the Willow River.

When McNally walked to his first class that fall of 1920, there were only three buildings on campus: the gymnasium, the science building, and a main building, which contained the old church, the monastery, the classrooms, and the student dorms.

John's fondness for the quiet campus set off in the middle of the rural countryside was apparent in his writings in the college newspaper, *The Record*. He'd been selected to the editorial staff and, from that post, he wrote pieces that offer great insight into his developing personal philosophy.

His essays showed the same willingness to embrace and consider the world he'd learned at home. One, called "Modern Exposure," explored the Jazz Age phenomenon of self-promotion (an art that John would master in the not-too-distant future). In another, he debunked what he called the "hypothesis" of evolution. But he did so, not from the position of most Catholics who "immediately shrink from the speaker [on evolution] in indignation." He did so, he said, from the position of "logical argumentation."

He also wrote a wonderful romp called "Hearts and Ink," a la Ring Lardner, in which the main character was a member of that burgeoning career path—sales. The piece even crossed gender lines in farcical fashion, as his protagonist pretended through a series of flowery letters to be a woman and his female love interest returned favor as a man.

McNally's poetry definitely swung toward the romantic, suggesting that Keats may have been a late-night companion in his St. John's dorm room. In his last piece, "Lake Sagatagan," he opens with:

Often my thirst for beauty have I slaked,
When floating gently mid the mists of night
Upon your bosom, while the tender lights
Of heaven gleamed; and in the limpid lake's
Clear depths then gleamed again, with airy shakes,
Like breeze-blown tapers lighting some strange rites,
Which water dwellers held just for my sake.
Oh, how I reveled in those strange delights.

John also reclaimed his academic success, probably because the isolation of the campus, the absence of members of the opposite sex, and the surrounding wilds made a turn inward possible. Roeser recorded:

> McNally did well in the classroom. He took a variety of subjects, from psychology to astronomy. He handled all well. He studied nothing long. He studied astronomy exactly one evening, completed the book, replaced it on the shelf, never referred to it again.

In the fall of 1920, John got his first taste of football. He was "drafted" into the school's intramural football program by one of the team's captains who approached him, telling him he'd been chosen. John didn't know what the guy was talking about and asked him, "How did you happen to pick me?" The captain replied that he'd seen John "running around the track one day," thought he was fast, and "might be pretty good at running the football."

Actually, John had become a bit of an athletic novelty on the St. John's campus that fall. According to Roeser:

> One evening McNally changed to football-type cleated shoes. He began to run in the football shoes, run and swerve as if his life depended on it. He ran and dodged every evening while his friends, sitting on the lawns, gaped. It was odd to see a guy running

down Collegeville Road in cleats at that time of the evening—odd and wonderful.

Football was strictly an intramural sport at this point; organized, intercollegiate gridiron play had disappeared from the campus ten years earlier. Really, the hiatus of football from the campus was no shock. Intercollegiate football had been around since just after the Civil War, but it was the Snidely Whiplash of popular sports as compared with its fair-haired counterpart, baseball. Football was a bone-crushing proposition, which proved even to be fatal at times. The publication of an annual death toll at season's end was fuel for the fire of the sport's critics. Between 1901 and 1907, 101 football deaths had been tallied.

Many universities had sensed the conflict between teaching higher values and watching members of their football team dragging their bruised and broken bodies across the campus, or worse yet, bearing the coffins of their fallen comrades. At St. John's, various *Record* editorials had denounced the sport. One, from November 1907, had used four pages to argue that football ran counter to the best interests of the college, did not promote loyalty to the school, and stirred up animosity between St. John's and other schools. It ended with the proclamation that with an intramural program, "Sports would then cease to be for the primary purpose of victory and would again become a means of recreation and amusement—the only legitimate reason for their existence." Nonetheless, St. John's intramural teams did keep track of the score for their games, suggesting that "recreation and amusement" might be sufficient in some circles but they couldn't replace good old-fashioned bragging rights.

All of this anti-football sentiment seemed to fit with the general athletic philosophy of the school (and the entire country at the time) as expressed in *Scoreboard: A History of Athletics at St. John's University:* "The star athlete, though always recognized and admired for his superior talents, has always been considered more as a member of the team than as an individual performer." The final decision on the presence of football was no doubt in the hands of Fr. Alcuin Deutsch, the University Rector at the time. In one of his poems, John McNally would describe then-Abbot Alcuin as "A Man of temper sweet, a son of peace." Any such man automatically had a problem with the roughhouse game of football.

"Football" from a page in John McNally's 1923 St. John's yearbook. There was a joy in the game that attracted young John McNally. Photograph obtained from and used with the permission of St. John's University.

To be sure, the Benedictine monks who started the college believed in physical activity. They'd brought with them the Spartan influence of the German gymnasium system. They'd started the school in the Middle of Nowhere, Minnesota in 1857. Physicality was an obvious and basic building block of existence; how else would they get their charges to cut and haul firewood, for instance? For recreational activity, however, baseball was already established.

John McNally now stood at about 5'10" and 150 pounds. He became known as the kid who ran everywhere, because he'd determined, on his own, to do so. The reputation clearly enhanced his attractiveness in the intramural draft. Following his stint at St. John's, there would be those who remembered John's "regular runs into the larger city of St. Cloud some seven miles away." The story is probably apocryphal; after all, St. Cloud was about twelve miles distant, and St. John's didn't encourage its students to take off on a whim for another town—even John McNally, who'd come to them "full of run" thanks to his excursions in New Richmond.

His football team that autumn was called the Cat's Pajamas, a popular phrase of the day suggesting something very "hip." John played tailback and his crew won the championship against five other teams. He told Hickok, "I'd never played football in my life. This guy thought I looked the right size to be a football player, I guess, so he chose me." It was a humble start of a football career that still ranks with the very best.

But John pitched himself into the new sport the same way he threw himself completely into any new pursuit—be it hopping trains or mastering

Shakespeare's sonnets. Roeser reported John's early work on the gridiron as self-driven and extensive:

> Between practice sessions, he raced by himself. He traced a path of cleats down to Collegeville Station and back. He remained to himself afternoons, rehearsing football, grasping the fundamentals, mastering the crude art. By himself, more than by extensive coaching, McNally learned how to plan elementary plays, to drop-kick, to run in twisting, crazy-legged fashion, to struggle when tackled, always to fall forward after dragging the tackler as far as he could.

In the fall of 1920, St. John's entered the Minnesota Intercollegiate Athletic Conference, made up of nine liberal arts colleges from around the state. The MIAC would promote "sportsmanlike competition between Minnesota colleges." St. John's was sure to field basketball and baseball teams for MIAC competition. What wasn't certain was the return of a football squad to do battle with the other schools. Because St. John's was also a prep school, not all of its athletes had technically graduated from high school and thus were ineligible for MIAC play. The school determined to field a prep squad to battle area high schools and develop a collegiate eleven to mix it up in the MIAC, but not as a full-fledged member of the conference. At least, not right away.

Football season gave way to basketball, and thirty athletes reported to St. John's ornate gymnasium. John McNally had never tried his hand at the hardwood sport, but he took to it like a horse to spring grass. Two-thirds of the students trying out were cut, yet John made the team. By the end of the season, the school newspaper, *The Record*, described him as a guy who "never played basketball before but was advancing fast." The team ended its season with a record of 8 wins and 6 losses. In his first attempt at basketball, John had become the starting center, thanks to some newfound height and personal tenacity.

As 1921 rolled around, John's success and popularity on campus were surging. His football and basketball triumphs behind him, he set his sights on the cinder oval. Track had also been on low flame on the back burner since its first appearance on campus in 1903. John was one of four men

McNally (front row center) thought basketball was his best sport. Photograph obtained from and used with the permission of St. John's University.

selected by the school's athletic director, Fr. Albert Heuring, to represent St. John's at the annual MIAC track meet at Northfield. According to *Scoreboard*, he was also "elected to the captaincy of the newly organized track team." In the MIAC state meet at St. Olaf that spring, John cleared a high jump of 5'6 ¹/₂" and took first place.

John's next step into the athletic arena came on the annual Memorial Field Day Celebration. *Scoreboard* called the field day a "truly colorful event":

> Faculty, students, parents and other relatives, visitors from the surrounding area, mixed together in lively camaraderie to cheer on their favorites. On some occasions even the college band paraded and led off contests with a lively marching tune. There was plenty of shouting and cheering as the spectators lined up alongside the track, urging on their favorites to muster up all the speed and power they possessed.

John was surely a boy in spring that day. He earned the most individual points over the day's events and was presented with the silver loving cup. In turn, John handed the trophy to his father. It would prove to be providential, as John's father was now suffering from melancholia brought on by ennui and advancing age. The joy was waning for the "keen raconteur." John told Hickok that John's father was bewildered by the change. "Having been in that natural high, that state of elation, all of his life, he simply didn't know how to cope with depression. He couldn't understand what was happening to him." It was a cause for concern for everyone else, as well. His co-workers at the New Richmond Roller Mills, his friends and relatives, and his wife all were puzzled by his sudden loss of vigor.

John told author Ralph Hickok that winning the loving cup was his most satisfying moment—more satisfying than any of the Packers' championships, more satisfying even than his induction into the Pro Football Hall of Fame. He presented that cup to his father as concrete proof of his now-realized athletic abilities. It could not turn the tide of his father's failing health, however. By summer, his father's depression had advanced to the point where his behavior became erratic. Suddenly, he was reported missing and John, Jr., raced home from visiting an aunt in the Twin Cities to help with the search. On August 21, his father's body was found in the Apple River, just west of New Richmond. Though it was never officially pronounced so, John McNally, Sr.'s, death was well understood to have been a suicide. He was buried in the Immaculate Conception cemetery.

To some, the death of his father seemed not to affect John. He returned to St. John's and picked up where he'd left off—academically and socially. However, his close friend, John Doar, would later suggest that the loss of his father when John was just shy of eighteen impacted him profoundly. "My first thought," John McNally told Ralph Hickok, "is that it was such a terrible tragedy, such a waste. I had a great admiration for him, I thought he was a great guy, and we were good friends. My second thought was, 'Now he can see me, he can watch everything I do, and he can see what a son-of-a-bitch I am.'"

Many years later, John would learn, reported Hickok, that his father had been kicked out of St. John's:

> I never had any idea, until I met this gas station owner in St. Cloud, who'd been a classmate of my father's. He told me all about it. According to him, my father got into a tobacco-spitting contest with another student, in a classroom. They were spitting for distance out the window. They got caught, and they were both expelled. Somehow, finding out about that made me feel better about my own academic accomplishments.

When the 1921 football season rolled around, several events had melded to launch John McNally even further on his football path. To be sure, he'd earned some accolades as the fleet-footed back on the Cat's Pajamas, and his exploits on the field day had turned some heads. St. John's was now also fully enrolled in the MIAC as a football school. But the death of his father also spurred him on. He had proven himself a clutch hitter, at least in the short term, and he had shown his father that those warm days on the front lawn hadn't gone unfulfilled.

His mother had also been honored. John had returned to his studious ways. He'd been selected for his post on *The Record* and was also a member of the yearbook staff. Eventually, he'd become a popular thespian, as well.

The 1921 football team was not successful. Despite John's contributions on both offense and defense, the squad took it on the nose against conference foes Hamline, St. Mary's, and Macalester, and was further humiliated by a high school team from Alexandria, which went on to take the state high school championship. The Fighting Johnnies did manage a defeat of St. Cloud Normal.

John McNally, *Quarter*

"What joy in spring it is to be a boy!" McNally's theatrics and joie de vivre drew others to him. He never seemed to take the game—whatever the game was—too seriously. Here he is as a St. John's football player. Photograph obtained from and used with the permission of St. John's University.

John had put in another respectable season at tailback and scored the season's first touchdown, the first for the school in conference play since 1910.

The basketball season was also a disappointment, with John anchoring the team at center. With a 7-6 record, the team placed fifth in the MIAC. In track, John did no better than 3rd place in the broad jump when he overstepped the take-off board by an inch. In the annual field day, he placed second to schoolmate Marcel Haines by four points. (Haines had taken second to John the year before.) Athletic firecrackers marked his sophomore year, not the explosion he'd enjoyed on the sports scene as a freshman.

The highlight of John's year was probably his mile run at the field day. He'd been told by a 'savvy' upperclassman to "follow close behind Brown [the favorite in the event] until in the last lap when he begins his 'kick'— then give it all you've got." McNally followed the advice, almost to the finish line. When Brown's kick wasn't forthcoming, John decided to take matters into his own hands and he shot past Brown with a burst. Brown had no kick in him, having exhausted his resources just staying in front of McNally. "It was quite a show!" *Scoreboard* reported. "Mac always had by a gift of nature a vivid sense of the dramatic!"

St. John's first year back in the MIAC conference was 1921. Like most years, the football season started off with promise and ended with philosophical assessments of what went wrong. John is in the back row, far left. Photograph obtained from and used with the permission of St. John's University.

That summer, John spent time in the Twin Cities, essentially interning for his uncle at the *Tribune*. He was becoming accustomed to all the cities had to offer and was still close enough to venture back home to New Richmond for some carefree days when he could.

The fall of 1922 was the start of John's last year at St. John's, at least for another three decades. (In between, he'd make his mark in the football world as the inimitable Johnny Blood.) On November 27, he turned eighteen.

For the '22 gridiron season, the school spruced up the natural bowl near the campus that served as a football and track facility; however, *Scoreboard* described that fall's pigskin campaign as "far from being a successful adventure into the MIAC football battles. St. John's lost all of its five scheduled conference games." They did win an early exhibition contest over Little Falls High School. *The Record* was especially brutal in its assessment:

Let the curtain be mercifully drawn over the most disastrous season in the annals of any sport at St. John's, and let the balm of future victories soothe the sting of these past defeats.

The basketball team didn't fare a lot better, ending with a 5–9 tally. It was a crazy season. Although the Fighting Johnnies outscored their opponents by a margin of 320 to 277. Their wins had been big, but their losses had been by the narrowest of margins. Still, John was named the all-conference center for scoring 95 of the team's 236 conference points. He'd also been elected captain of the team, though the process was a crazy one. Both John and Tony Gornick were returning lettermen, but the first two months of the season were spent deciding who would serve as captain. "As each was too modest to vote for himself, they flipped a coin for the office. Mac won the toss. Congratulations, Mac!" said *The Record.*

Track season found a team without a coach and, as a result, without a team. So John's athletic swan song would have to be performed in the annual Memorial Field Day. He was also determined to try his hand at baseball, a pursuit that had sat idle in his heart since those days with his father on the corner of West Second Street and Montana Avenue.

Thirteen events were slated for the Field Day, and John entered twelve of them. "The only event in which he did not compete," recorded *Scoreboard,* "was the shot put, possibly because it conflicted with one of the other events that he preferred." With his rival, Marcel Haines, off to medical school, it was John's day to shine.

Of his twelve events, John took first place in the 120-yard high hurdles, 220-yard low hurdles, high jump, broad jump, mile run, half-mile run, 440-yard dash, pole vault, and discuss throw. He took second in the 100-yard dash, 220-yard dash, and javelin throw. He had set new school records in the mile and half mile, and earned the silver loving cup once again as high point man for the day.

But John's greatest athletic feat, the one that only a clutch hitter could pull off, came in a late-season baseball game. John determined that he was going to earn letters in four sports. In doing so, he'd become St. John's very first man to win the distinction. He'd already amassed letters in football, basketball, and track. At this late date, baseball was his final option.

John set his sights on pitching a game, though he'd never done this in the past. Hickok records that John went to Sunday mass a few days before the game with a baseball and Christy Matthewson's book on pitching in hand. There in church that day, under the watchful eye of the Great Umpire, he began practicing the proper finger positions for the various pitches. It must have done some good.

Three days later, he toed the mound against MIAC opponent Macalester. John gave up just three hits and led St. John's to a victory over its rivals from St. Paul. He'd closed out his career at St. John's a smashing success, a "clutch hitter" as it were, from the pitching mound. He'd done it in his own style—a combination of self-determination, sharp wits, keen study, and natural ability. He'd learned a little about being a clutch hitter and a performer. It was time to jump off the train, run down the tracks, and climb onto another.

He'd also been celebrated for the first time in the pages of his hometown newspaper, the *New Richmond News and Republican-Voice*. It had been compelled to give John some ink, it said, since the *Minneapolis Journal* had devoted "a three column head and a full length halftone of John in athletic regalia."

The Minneapolis paper asked the question, "Is there anything Mac can't do?" From there, the *News* embraced its homeboy as a regional hero, concluding that McNally was considering Notre Dame next year but that St. John's fans were hoping he would change his mind.

John's own assessment of his newfound athleticism was relayed in later years to Richard Whittingham:

> I was a runt as a kid, but by the time I got into St. John's I'd grown up to be a spike. I suppose I never got to be any heavier than 165 pounds while I was there, but I'd been toughened up by working on the farm there in Wisconsin. I still worked there in the summers while I was going to St. John's. And also I was about the fastest guy around.

That John McNally made friends and earned admirers at St. John's is borne out in the pages of his last yearbook, the 1923 *Sagatagan*. John himself had overseen production of the annual as editor-in-chief.

"I like your philosophy of life, Mac. 'Let the world spin on forever.'" — John Pat Broderick.

"John, thanks for letting me be your second. I hope to be it in everything

John (left) was popular at St. John's. "I like your philosophy of life, Mac. 'Let the world spin on forever,'" John Pat Broderick wrote in his friend's last yearbook. Photograph obtained from and used with the permission of St. John's University.

when I get out in the world." — Wilfred Engel.

"Here's to you super man and super good fellow. I wish we could have another year together, Jack. Keep on sailing. With all sincerity." — Tom "Doc" McKeon.

"Here's to a great athlete, John V. McNally. Hoping you have the same spirit all thru life as you have had here. Also hoping you get by big at Notre Dame." — Ed Powers.

"'Two men looked thru their prison bars. One saw mud, the other stars.' — Stevenson. The latter always applied to you, John, and is one of your great attributes that attracts the multitudes including myself."— Ralph E. Hanson.

Near his Glee Club picture, Hanson also wrote, "Dear John: Always remember with me our day dreaming, our deep philosophy and evolution theorys [sic].— Hans." Hanson would factor into the John McNally legend shortly, at that very point when it shifted into the Johnny Blood legend.

McNally had come to St. John's, wrote Tom Roeser, "an individualist, a doer of things unconsciously different." He was leaving the same way, now much surer that his individualism was also his ticket to the world and to his relationship with others. The train was beginning to roll. The stars were shining brightly.

Chapter ③

Blood is Born (and Borne)
(1923–1925)

Progress is the fruit of necessity and dissatisfaction, not of comfort and content. The watchword of the young man should be Progress; and where shall the youth, as he gazes upon his future wrapped in a garb of dreams and mist and visions, where shall he strive to advance?

— John V. McNally

John described himself as "precocious" as a child, "a quick study." Intellectually, he'd mastered everything that came his way. But athletically, he had been too small to participate in team sports. At St. John's, it all came together. His junior yearbook, which he edited, was testimony to his achievements in academics, literary and forensic clubs, *and* sports. The many inscriptions of his schoolmates also spoke of the esteem in which they held him and their clear sense that this was a rising star, a young man with a self-designed philosophy that would meet the world on his own terms, taking from it what he deemed important.

During the summer of 1923, two activities would preoccupy John's time. First, his New Richmond friends and relatives encouraged him to apply for a Rhodes Scholarship. He did but was turned down. His brother Jim told author Ralph Hickok that the family learned via a Minneapolis-area selector that "John had scored the highest in every category. But they felt he was too young." After all, 19-year-old John had not actually graduated from college, despite his many accomplishments. He was encouraged to reapply after obtaining his degree.

With that, John set his sights on the University of Notre Dame. For a young Midwestern Irish–Catholic man with some football skills, Notre Dame was the mecca, and John was the hardy pilgrim. Football at the South Bend school had taken on a new charm under the direction of one Knute Rockne, a former Notre Dame grid star himself. On Rockne's roster were four pretty decent footballers as well: Harry Stuhldreher, Don Miller, Jim Crowley, and Elmer Layden. In 1920, these four junior backs would become known to the sporting world as the Four Horsemen.

Rule changes in 1912 had encouraged the forward pass, and its practitioners had brought a new flair to the game. Running was okay, but it was typically plodding and slow. On the other hand, tossing the pigskin into the air and hauling it in well downfield invited the theatrical. The drama was right up John's alley, and Rockne was one of the most dedicated disciples of the pass.

John also had a keen interest in Notre Dame basketball, a sport he actually considered his best. As the anchorman on his St. John's teams, he'd been able to draw his zest for the dramatic together with his halcyon athletic skills. Literally, he'd been the center of attention. But could he make the Irish team against equally skilled talent from across the nation? Unfortunately, he would never get a chance to find out.

Knute Rockne was on the cutting edge of football technology in the 1920s. Photograph obtained from and used with the permission of Jim Jameson.

"Success in sports at St. John's," he told Ralph Hickok, "was not really a very big thing. Oh, it was gratifying. But I had no illusions about it. It was high school sports. . . . I thought I would find out, at Notre Dame, if I really had any skill worth bothering about. And, of course, I was still looking for a degree."

John turned out for football and was immediately pulled from the group of tailbacks and switched to tackle. Tackle? Back in the 1890s, a tackle could earn some glory, but by 1923 he was just a guy lost in the line, with little chance of distinguishing himself other than laying out an opposing player. There wasn't much jazz to be had at the tackle spot, and this was, after all, the jazz age.

John told the assistant coach, George Keogan, his take on things. "A tackle's job is to seek contact. A halfback's job is to avoid contact. I think my talent, if I have any, lies in avoiding contact."

At that point, John's football career at Notre Dame was over. Also nearly over was his enrollment at the university. His one contribution to Notre Dame football and to the legend of the Four Horsemen was writing Harry Stuhldreher's English poetry papers for him. John spent that fall playing football for the South Bend YMCA.

"A halfback's job is to avoid contact. I think my talent, if I have any, lies in avoiding contact." John at Notre Dame. Photograph obtained from and used with the permission of John Doar.

He also took an apartment off campus, which was a clear violation of university rules. The immortal George Gipp had done the same thing, but John McNally hadn't ascended to anywhere near immortal status at Notre Dame. He described his apartment-keeping as far more about convenience than about romance, though he admitted to using it "maybe once a month" for that purpose, as well. Meanwhile, he maintained his dorm room for appearance's sake.

St. Patrick's Day, 1924, rolled around and John got himself embroiled in a revolving street celebration with some friends. One thing led to another and, as the crowd swelled, a streetcar was turned on its side. John was the only one caught. Unlike his compadres, he hadn't even tried to run. Rather than at the hands of the police, his punishment would come from the college disciplinarian—quite likely a worse fate. John was suspended from school for two months, essentially ending his Notre Dame days. He declined the opportunity to mitigate his fate by ratting out some of his accomplices. Nor did he wait out his suspension and resume his studies. Across his transcript, someone wrote "Gone—Never to Return!" And he never did. Thus he became what he described as a "double-dipped dropout." His family was no doubt disappointed.

That winter, John stayed in South Bend working as a clerk, typing in the office of the Studebaker plant. He also played basketball for the "Y." But he was getting itchy. It was time to hit the road once again. And he did, literally. This time it wasn't on a train but on a motorcycle. According to Hickok, the bike in question was a used, four-cylinder Ace that cost John $125.

For the trip, he hooked up with a hot, married blonde he'd met at a dance and taken to his apartment. The woman was 18 years old and had a couple of children. Coincidentally or not, John's sisters, Lucille and Honor, were sailing to Europe and it afforded him an opportunity to see them off. It also afforded him, for the first time ever, a ticket to the wide-open road. Everything pointed to a motorcycle trip to the East Coast, and off they went.

First they motored west, into Chicago, where John bought a suit. With no extra money, they spent the night on a park bench. The next day, John pointed the Ace eastward and squeezed the accelerator. A few hours into the excursion, they stopped in Fort Wayne, Indiana, where the girl's parents lived and where her children were staying. Her father was a member of the Ku Klux Klan, she told John, and he'd best not mention that he was Catholic or went to Notre Dame. In fact, he'd best not use his real name. They spent the night and headed onward.

From there, the trip was an evolving, catch-as-catch-can adventure. There were more nights sleeping on park benches, some pawned jewelry, and a few odd jobs. There were sparks flying between John's knees, caused by static electricity, as they raced out of the Cumberland Mountains. "Like St. Elmo's fire," he told Hickok. "Here I was, a novice motorcyclist, rolling down a mountainside with this dame hanging on behind me for dear life, and suddenly I'm radioactive or something. But we made it."

On at least one occasion, John and the blonde split up. Tight on funds, he stashed the Ace and resorted to a skill he'd learned back in New Richmond: hopping trains. It was on one such train that John expanded his knowledge of train operation, though not to his immediate advantage. Some trains, he would learn, took on water "on the fly," and John had stashed himself in the blind baggage compartment where he found himself drenched by the spray.

He showed up in Baltimore to see an aunt and uncle and, perhaps, replenish his wallet. His cousin, Clarence J. Mulrooney, remembered the sudden visit:

> His calling card was his valise thrown through the open transom at noon when we were out to lunch with the office door locked. He returned later. He went to Washington, D.C., ran up the Washington Monument and down, took in the sights and then was off to New York. A few days later, my assistant, Mr. Teufel, said to me that he had bumped into my cousin John the night before near the B & O office building. His face was black with coal dust, which he explained he acquired riding the blind baggage from New York.

Through his family connections, John worked for about a month in New York as a stereotyper. Then, he collected his abandoned motorcycle in Virginia and went on his way; this time without his blonde passenger, to whom he had

John's carefree, adventurous spirit joined forces with a circa-1920 Ace Motorcycle (like this one) and a married blonde, following his sudden departure from Notre Dame. Photograph obtained from and used with the permission of Ace Motocross Club of Modena, NY.

sent money so she could make her own way home. He hooked up with old friends from Notre Dame and his sister Helen who was at summer school at Radcliffe College. He pinched most of them for funds, leaving worthless checks in his wake and hoping to get back to New Richmond before the checks did.

All told, it was a defining adventure for John—his first foray as a full-fledged vagabond. He was just twenty years old and he'd gone on a free-wheeling, cross-country tear. He'd figured it out as he went, using his cleverness and skills along the way. It was a wonderful metaphor for what was to come. He told Hickok, "It seems incredible to me now. When I think about it, it's just the way the hippies are. I was an easy rider. Maybe I was the first hippie, just forty years ahead of my time. I was drifting along, in the sense that I was looking for my lifestyle, as they say nowadays."

John spent the next few months at home in the big McNally house. Of course, it was much emptier now—just John, James, Margaret, and their mother. Relatives began to pummel John with ideas about his future. They figured one wayward motorcycle trip should be enough for anyone. It was time to focus on the future. His family was well-connected enough to offer some options and opportunities. As old friend John Doar said, "They just wanted him to find some balance, to maximize his talents."

His mother felt a career in law was just the thing to combine his sharp mind, his ability to express himself, and his dramatic leanings. She sent him to his Uncle Will McNally's law office on Main Street to study. There, he sat with a young Warren P. Knowles, reading law books. But John told Hickok, "I didn't care for it at all. At least, not going at it that way, which was already outmoded, anyway." Within a few weeks, he was back at home with a law career off the table. Knowles, however, stayed and was eventually elected governor of Wisconsin.

Next, John went off to Minneapolis to try his hand full-time at the *Tribune*. Again, the prevailing thought was, "John is good with words, and his wits would make him a good businessman." He'd already had some practical experience working on the yearbook and *The Record* at St. John's, and he'd put in a little time at the "*Trib*" the previous two summers. He even landed a job at the paper for his old St. John's buddy, Ralph Hanson.

John worked hard at the *Tribune*. At one point, his uncle offered him the key to the main office—ownership of the paper—if he was willing to work his way up. John told Hickok that his response to his uncle's offer was less than gracious. "I was too steamed up about the new freedom of being an adult to think about owning a newspaper someday," he said.

Working his way up meant starting at the bottom. With some experience as a stereotyper from his short time in New York, John started there, along with Hanson. The two of them would haul the stereotypes—heavy printing plates—about the newspaper offices. Old ones had to be melted down and used again, and new ones were set in the presses to print that day's edition. It was the kind of labor that helped tone muscles.

One day at work, the two of them saw a small item in the paper. It was an invitation to able-bodied men to try out for a semi-pro football team, the East 26th Street Liberties. Five other teams were also looking for men and, along with the Liberties, would form a citywide league for play that fall. Since the Liberties were the team closest to the newspaper's downtown offices, John and Ralph decided to head over to the Liberties' practice field after work that day.

Both had a year of college eligibility left that they wanted to protect. John told Richard Whittingham that at that point he still entertained the thought that "maybe one of those days I might be going back to Notre Dame, in the unlikely event they'd have me; but still it was a possibility." John also had a hunch that the Liberties might play some games out of state, particularly in western Wisconsin, increasing the risk that "John McNally" might be recognized. In order to protect their eligibility, they would have to use fake names, something guys in their situation had done countless times over the years.

Ever since 1905, when Teddy Roosevelt had put out his five-point plan for improving the safety of the rough game of football, things like eligibility mattered. Before that, a man could do time on the gridiron for the local semi-pro team, the college team, even the high school team. If he wanted, he could play games for all three the same day. A guy named John K. Brallier had done pretty much that. But now, things were very different, and if John was going to return to South Bend, playing semi-pro ball would slam the door on that possibility.

At the end of work that day, they hopped on John's Ace and headed south on Hennepin Avenue, still unsure of what names they would give the Liberties' manager when they showed up for tryouts. They were, however, set on using aliases. Seven blocks later, John swung the motorcycle east on 7th Street, heading toward Nicollet Avenue, which would take them to the Liberties' practice field. On 7th Street, they passed the Garrick Theater and John looked up at the marquee. It read, "Rudolph Valentino Star of *Blood and Sand* in *Monsieur Beaucaire*." "That's it!" John yelled back to Ralph. "I'll be Blood and you be Sand."

"If Olsen and Johnson had been playing," John later told Ralph Hickok, "I guess we would have been John Olsen and Ralph Johnson." At that point, Hickok suggested that "John Olsen" wouldn't have stood the test of time like "Johnny Blood" has. "Probably not," John told him. Hickok wondered whether John had realized at the time that Blood was the more colorful name:

> No, not consciously. But I can't speak for my subconscious. The idea was probably lurking around in there somewhere. You never really know what your subconscious is doing, and it's always up to something.

Passing the Garrick Theater in Minneapolis, John McNally created his most famous moniker—"Johnny Blood." Photograph obtained from and used with the permission of the Minnesota Historical Society.

Today, the Garrick operates as the Music Box Theater, and the Liberties' practice field is still an odd-shaped, innocuous stretch of open ground in a factory neighborhood with Minneapolis traffic humming in the background. The two tangible elements of this fantastic tale remain in place, as they were that late-summer afternoon in 1924.

As "Blood" and "Sand," McNally and Hanson both made the team and spent that fall playing hard-nosed football for the Liberties. With John back in his old spot at tailback, the Liberties won the league championship.

John described his Liberties teammates to Hickok as follows:

> About twenty guys came out—cops, truck drivers, a couple of kids just out of high school, a few guys like Ralph and me, who'd played some college ball and just wanted to keep playing.

Like most of the semi-pro teams of the day, the Liberties held night practices, with a floodlight mounted on a pole to beat back the autumn darkness. During the day, the guys worked to support families and help pay for their football equipment. Spectators were charged admission, and after expenses were met the two teams would split up the proceeds, if there were any. Often, the visiting team would get some kind of guarantee from the home team, but that wasn't a sure thing, either. For their troubles, John (McNally) Blood and Ralph (Hanson) Sand were paid $6 a game.

At season's end, the Liberties were undefeated and John was selected as a starter on a city league all-star team that played against the Minneapolis Marines, a football

Possibly the first shot of "Johnny Blood" in action in the 1924 Minneapolis Park Board league. John's team—the East 26th Street Liberties—won the championship that year. Photograph obtained from and used with the permission of John Doar.

crew that had clawed its way out of the ranks of teams like the Liberties to join the National Football League. Their reputation from the old days was vaunted. However, against the national powerhouses in the NFL, they stumbled. Their 1924 record stood at 0-6. It would prove to be the Marines' last year in the national league ranks. Still, they represented a step up in class for Johnny Blood and his teammates. After the game, the Marines' coach approached John about playing pro ball the next year as a Marine. As it turned out, John would indeed find his way into NFL—as a Duluth Eskimo, however. And it would take two more years.

John next set his sights on a short career as a pugilist. And why not? He'd never tried it before. The autumn of 1924 had drifted into the winter of 1925, and a young man of twenty-one had to have some way to pass the time.

"It started with this guy ribbing me," John told Hickok. "The press-room boss, a big guy named Billy Hoak, who was a real boxing fan. 'So you think you're an athlete? Well, there's a little guy named Pete Sarmiento who'd just kill you.'" John told Hickok his curiosity was piqued. "It was probably true," he admitted, "but I could never just accept something on theory, it had to be proved to me."

John took on a trainer, Ernie Fliegel, who spent at least part of his day at Labe Safro's gym on Hennepin Avenue. En route, he passed the "*Trib*" building at the corner of 4th Street and Nicollet. John began pressing Fliegel to show him how to box. Fliegel first asked John why a rich kid would want to fight. John could hardly impress Fliegel with the idea that it was a flight of fancy. He insisted on the seriousness of his intentions, and Fliegel invited him over to the gym.

Fliegel wanted John to train for a couple of months and then they'd see about an actual fight. John would have none of it. He wasn't interested in a full-time boxing career, just a quick study's introduction to the sport. Obviously, he'd bring his usual sharp focus and determination to the chore. "Inside a week," Fliegel said, "Johnny had developed a beautiful jab, a way of slipping punches and smart countering."

John's one and only bout was at the Gayety Theater, at 103 North Washington. The Gayety hosted vaudeville acts as well as fights. Sarmiento had another fight that night, and Fliegel had to pull every string he could to get his untested fighter on the bill at all. John, who wasn't interested in working his way up the fight ladder, stepped into the ring with Johnny Anderson, a middleweight champ who hadn't lost in fifty fights. John battled Anderson over three rounds, essentially beating him. But Fliegel told John not to go into the fourth round, and Anderson was handed the decision. The downstairs dressing room was chaos. Fliegel was being back-slapped for discovering this new talent. He went to tell John that they'd get back to training in a few days, and John said, "I'm not going to box anymore. I only wanted to find out whether I can fight. Now I've got everything I want out of boxing." With that, he was back to his work as a stereotyper.

Years later, a conversation took place over John's brief boxing career between three fishermen on Minnesota's Lake of the Woods. In the boat were George Strickler, sports editor of the *Chicago Tribune*, a friend of his, and a former amateur boxer.

"Impossible," said the former boxer after hearing the story. "It couldn't happen. There's no way that a kid can fight that well in his first fight."

Strickler replied:

> You didn't know Johnny Blood. He was the most gifted athlete I've ever seen. He could be a master of any sport he undertook. As a fighter he was ahead of the others from the moment he pulled on the gloves because he had the athletic skills which would give him that head start on natural ability alone.

In the late summer of 1925, John's football plans consisted of nothing more than hanging around in the Twin Cities and trying out for the Marines in September, if they had regrouped after their 1924 debacle. If that didn't work out, he could always return to the Liberties. Then, in August, football came calling on him.

The Iron Range of Michigan's Upper Peninsula was known for one thing: mining. In 1925, mining was tough and dangerous work. Deadly, in fact. The miners up there also took to football in a big way. With all the raw violence of the sport in the 1920s, it seemed like a Sunday afternoon parlor game compared with busting rock thousands of feet under the earth's surface. Every town in the "U.P." had a team—Negaunee, Bessemer, Stambaugh, Iron River, and Iron Mountain, to name a few. Ironwood was no different.

And so it was that a couple of members of the Ironwood Miners team ventured to the *Tribune* offices one day, seeking the football talents of one Johnny Blood. They'd caught wind of his running ability via the gridiron grapevine and were willing to pay him a whopping $60 a game.

Behind him, John left a family that was more than a little upset. He'd finally put a year into a solid job and lying right on the table in front of him was ownership of the *Tribune*. What was he thinking?

John explained his side of things to Hickok:

> I wanted to be able to do something I enjoyed and something that would leave me enough leisure time to do other things that I enjoyed. The family, I'm sure, thought I was being lazy, being afraid of work. But that wasn't it. I've worked hard at a lot of jobs—I worked hard at being a stenographer. What I wanted was freedom, and freedom meant, to me, being allowed to choose what I wanted to do.

John's relationship with his mother had been shaky ever since the death of his father four years earlier. Now he was turning his back on guaranteed success—in order to do what? To play professional football— a calling that ranked just slightly above that of bank robber or circus freak. And where? In some God-forsaken mining town!

It would take John more than a few years to work his way back into the family's good graces. Perhaps they just got used to his vagabond ways and crossed off the list of respectable professions he might have pursued. After all, he wasn't really John McNally anymore. He was Johnny Blood. The Ironwood team hadn't offered sixty bucks a game to a precocious small kid from New Richmond named John McNally, but to a guy who could draw fans to their games and help them pile up victories.

"This was quite a training ground," John told Ralph Hickok of his football days in Ironwood. He added:

> The games were rough as hell, but the parties after the games were even rougher. Both teams would usually go over to Hurley [Wisconsin] to drink, and the brawls that started during the game would resume right where they'd been left off.

John learned all that over just three games with the Miners. Then, suddenly, he was contacted by the Milwaukee Badgers of the NFL and offered the princely sum of $75 a game. He took it and ran, quite literally, as the Badgers' halfback. Like that, John had made the jump into the big time, and the Miners were left to party, play football, and fight in his wake.

The pass had "opened up" the game on football fields all across the United States in the mid-1920s.
Photograph obtained from and used with the permission of the Minnesota Historical Society.

The stories of the National Football League's founding at Ralph Hay's Hupmobile dealership on the hot, sweaty night of September 17, 1920, are the stuff of legend. Beer and football stories are said to have flowed freely as the league's organizers hammered out a set of by-laws. They had a couple of basic goals: first, to establish some uniformity in terms of equipment, rules, and scheduling, and second, to stop the uncivilized warfare between them as they bid for the services of star players. What they were organizing would be called the American Professional Football Association. It would not become the NFL until June 1922.

The league had seen its first action in the fall of 1920 and then promptly fell flat to the floor in a worthless heap. The loosely constructed organization imploded thanks to scheduling difficulties, the struggle of individual member teams to stay afloat, infighting over players jumping from team to team, and the use of college players—the bane of every football league before it. Controversy over who had actually won the 1920 championship didn't help either. It wasn't until the following year that the Akron Pros were awarded the Brunswick-Balke Collender loving cup, recognizing their "world's professional championship."

In April 1921, league members poked the pile to see whether it still had life and then resumed under the direction of Joe Carr. Even if he did drive the league like a stern stepfather, Carr introduced some key ideas that helped it breathe again. He gave each franchise a territory, thereby building a local fan base. He also determined team standings at the end of the season, including an eventual champion based on winning percentage.

Over the 1920s, fifty-four teams signed on to NFL membership. Today, only four of those teams remain: the Arizona Cardinals, the Chicago Bears, the Green Bay Packers, and the New York Giants. The Milwaukee Badgers would join the NFL in 1922 and field teams through the 1926 season. The team's best record would come in 1923 when it posted a 7–2–3 mark. Along the way, the team would sign class players like Fritz Pollard and Paul Robeson (two of the league's first black players), and Jimmy Conzleman.

John took a natural shine to California and Catalina Island. Photograph obtained from and used with the permission of John Doar.

Despite picking up Johnny Blood for the remainder of the 1925 season, the Badgers did not fare very well, losing all six of their games. In a game against the Akron Pros, John was lined up against Olympic sprinter and broad jumper Sol Butler. John shot past Butler, hauled in a pass, and outran Butler to score a 55-yard touchdown. He had now proven himself against the best.

After the six losses, John caught a train home for New Richmond and was enjoying his hometown as it prepared for the approaching Christmas holidays. Then, as a favor to Chicago Cardinals owner Chris O'Brien, Badgers manager John Dunn called together as many of his players as he could for one more game. John was not one of them. To round out his squad, Dunn secured four high school players. The Badgers, such as they were, would play a game against the Cardinals to help the Cards pad their season-ending record and pay back some shenanigans of the Pottsville Maroons. And so they did.

The December 10 contest ended 59-0 in favor of the Cardinals. As a result of the drubbing, the Badgers suffered more than embarrassment. At the league's winter meeting, Carr dropped the hammer on the Milwaukeans. Team owner Ambrose L. McGurk was fined $500 and ordered to sell the team within 90 days, and never darken the NFL doorstep again. Dunn was stripped of his position and also barred from the league for life.

With the team in disarray, John realized that his life in the NFL—if it was to continue—would find him traveling once again. That winter, he ventured to California for a little R & R. On Catalina Island, he worked as a bouncer and a "stick" man, handling the dice at the craps table. He told Ralph Hickok that he wasn't sure why he went to Catalina, but he offered a thought:

> I suspect that Avalon had something to do with it. Avalon is the only real city on the island and, of course, in the King Arthur stories it's the place where heroes went when they were dead. That probably in some way influenced me—I guess I figured it was the right place for a pro football player to go after the season.

One night, the customers had won a considerable amount of money and John asked the owner how the house could survive after a series of big losses. The answer found its way into John's ever-evolving philosophy:

> We win over the long run, because the rules of the game are such that the players win 47% of their bets and the house wins 53% of the bets, and that margin is what supports us and ruins the bettor in the long run. Monte Carlo and Catalina remain and the bettors die broke. We go with the percentage, and they go against it.

Chapter 4

The Vagabond Halfback Finds Green Bay (1926–1929)

I think football was an escape from another kind of life, and I enjoyed it so thoroughly I was always congratulating myself that I was able to find an escape so tolerable to me. To maximize my life.
— John V. McNally

John was now twenty-two years of age. With New Richmond as his anchor, he'd drifted around looking for something that made sense to him. He'd streaked across his hometown's sky and left so quickly, no one really knew him. He'd gone to three colleges and left his mission uncompleted at all of them. He'd torn up the highway on a motorcycle, heading for parts unknown. He'd hoisted stereotypes at two different newspapers, the plates reflecting a different story every day. He'd found an alias, Johnny Blood, thereby allowing him to live somewhere between fame and anonymity as long and as often as he wanted.

John's next excursion in the NFL would be playing for the Duluth Eskimos. It was a long way, in both distance and concept, from the warm environs of California and Catalina Island. The Eskimos franchise was probably the most colorful to ever do battle in the NFL; they were often called a "team of vagabonds." Because of their long schedule and the fact that they played most of their games on the road, sportswriter Grantland Rice dubbed them the "Iron Men of the North." John would connect with them partway through the 1926 season, after leaving the Badgers. He was now a traveling halfback on a traveling team.

Duluth, Minnesota, had fielded an NFL team, the Duluth Kelleys, since 1923. The Kelleys mostly mixed it up with the other town teams of the Minnesota–Michigan Iron Range, but once in a while they'd head off to face an NFL team somewhere in the Midwest. In 1923, they played the Green Bay Packers, losing 10-0. But the Kelleys aggregation had been flagging. At the end of the 1925 season, for the nominal sum of one dollar, the franchise was handed over to its voluntary secretary-treasurer, Ole Haugsrud, as payment or punishment. The team's name was changed to the Eskimos.

In 1926, Ole pulled off a *coup d'etat*. He signed Ernie Nevers, the most promising player coming out of college that year, to a contract. To be sure, Haugsrud had done some nifty bargaining. He matched an offer of $15,000 that Nevers was considering from a team in the American Football League and sweetened the pot with a percentage of the gate receipts. The fact that Nevers had graduated from high school in Superior, Wisconsin, with Haugsrud didn't hurt, either. The addition of Nevers made the Eskimos a force to be reckoned with. As John McNally often stated, "Ernie Nevers was the star. No, he was the team."

(Left) The Duluth Eskimos were more like a traveling freak show than an NFL team. They would parade through opposing towns in parkas on their way to the football field. Photograph obtained from and used with the permission of the Green Bay Packers Hall of Fame.

(Right) Ole Haugsrud toured his Duluth Eskimos over 17,000 miles during the 1926 season. Photograph obtained from and used with the permission of the Green Bay Packers Hall of Fame.

The problem for the Eskimos was that they were located so far north in such a small town, and the NFL wanted them to travel rather than host games. And travel they did. Between September 6, 1926, and February 5, 1927, the Eskimos played twenty-nine games—fifteen exhibition games and fourteen league contests. Only one of those games was at home on Duluth's old West Side Field. During one eight-day stretch, they played five games in five different locales.

Nevers was a football phenom, touching the ball on every offensive play from his fullback position in the double-wing formation. He sat out just twenty-nine minutes over the fourteen league games that season. Like other early players such as Curly Lambeau, George Halas, and Red Grange, he was a Renaissance football man who could run, pass, catch, and kick. He also played defense with abandon. John McNally, now toting around the moniker Johnny Blood, was rapidly becoming equally talented and diversified.

Completing the Eskimos roster were several quality Duluth- and Superior-area players, as well as the highly touted guards Jimmy Manion and Walt Kiesling. The rest were unremarkable, though nearly all had some college football experience. There were never more than sixteen players on the team. During games, Haugsrud and team manager Dewey Scanlon actually wore uniforms to make it look like there were more players, though they seldom got on the field. John suggested to Richard Whittingham that most of the Eskimos "weren't necessarily very good football players, but they were rugged and strong, a different breed."

The Eskimos tallied 17,000 miles that season, by every means of conveyance, and chalked up a 19–7–3 record. They also racked up about $4,000 per game for Haugsrud and his team, and gate receipts sometimes topped $8,000. Of course, most of that went to Nevers. The other players, including John, were paid $75 for a win, $65 for a tie, and $50 for a loss.

Haugsrud liked John as a pass receiver, citing his basketball experience. "John did something no other pass receiver of the time could do," he told Ralph Hickok.

> He always kept his body between the ball and the defensive man, and he used his body, his elbows, his shoulders, everything, to protect the ball, just like a good rebounder does. We knew, even if he was covered, we could throw him an alley-oop pass—we didn't

call it that, then, but that's what it was—and he'd probably come down with it.

Haugsrud also suggested to Hickok that it was Blood who often kept the whole thing going. "John would make a joke or two, or start clowning around, and everybody would smile and relax, just like that. It was like the sun coming out. He was always loose, and he helped the rest of us loosen up, too."

The Eskimos wore distinctive mackinaws with a large white igloo on them along with the team name. The same emblem was on their luggage and equipment trunks. It made a great impression on the fans and players in the towns where they showed up to do gridiron battle.

Despite the matching outfits, it was a rag-tag, hand-to-mouth existence, just as it was for most other football outfits of the day. Haugsrud struggled to collect his money from the other team's manager and to keep his players satisfied and in line. One of the players he seemed to struggle with most was Johnny Blood. "Johnny and the rest of them drank from the time the ball-game was over almost until the next one started," he told Hickok.

With this much time on the road, John was at his most footloose and fancy-free. His legend was beginning to take shape, with every story finding its rightful place in the Johnny Blood book of wine, women, and song.

There was the story of the man-versus-dog race before the Eskimos played the Racine Tornadoes. A speakeasy owner said his German shepherd could run twice as fast as any football player. The Eskimos nominated John to find out, and put up $75. The dog started on one goal line, enticed by a big steak at the other end of the field. Johnny Blood started at the fifty and crossed the goal line before the dog hit midfield. The tale doesn't say whether John got the steak. The dog's owner then suggested double or nothing over the game, and the Eskimos cleaned up, 21-0, on the heels of Blood's three touchdown receptions.

There was the time the team stayed at the Allerton Hotel in Cleveland with games set against three Ohio teams. Also staying there were the Marx Brothers and Max Sennett's Bathing Beauties. The men and women were assigned to alternating floors. Everything was at a point of homeostasis until Blood commandeered the elevator and rode it to one of the women's floors. Haugsrud and Nevers finally captured Blood and sent him to his room, but not before chaos worthy of the Marx Brothers had ensued.

There was the game against the St. Louis Gunners a few weeks later when Johnny Blood broke open for an easy score. The trouble was that he decided to stop and wait for the rest of the football menagerie to catch up. At the point where some Gunners were about to catch him and take him to the ground, he unexpectedly pitched the ball to a teammate, Paul Fitzgibbons, and laid a block into two Gunners while Fitzgibbons scored.

John's greatest moment in the sun—well, actually under the street-light—probably came on a snowy Thanksgiving evening in Buffalo. The game had been cancelled due to the weather, so the Eskimos decided to make the best of things and celebrate the holiday. Three times that evening Haugsrud had to shag John back up to his room following an escape. The first time, he was holding court on a street corner telling the crowd of his intentions to become the country's greatest mile runner. Haugsrud locked him in his room. Following a window-ledge escape with some bed sheets, Haugsrud took away John's clothes. The last straw came as John crawled out the transom in his roommate's ill-fitting suit. Finally, captured again, two team members held him down until he fell asleep. Later, John explained that, besides Thanksgiving, it was also two days after his birthday and he hadn't had time to celebrate that either.

Haugsrud liked to tell a couple of other "Blood stories." He said that John was clearly "the most colorful character on the Eskimos squad." His top player was "truly brilliant, both physically and mentally, but a trifle unpredictable."

One story revolved around John and Cobb Rooney going to a Chinese museum in San Francisco. John came home with a wealth of material, wrote a story, and sold it, said Haugsrud, "for several hundred dollars." Another time, John and Cobb took a couple of girls out to dinner, then went to a cab-stand to secure a ride home. They found a cab, but no cab driver. So John drove the girls home and returned the cab to its original spot, pinning a dollar to the steering wheel.

There was the night before a game with the Pottsville Maroons when John, Cobb Rooney, and Walt Kiesling went out to find a speakeasy. It turned out to be the local fire station. The three football men joined in as "visiting firemen" and got themselves pretty extinguished. John and Cobb decided to see who was the better fighter. At one point, John took a good swing at Cobb and put his fist into the brick wall of the firehouse. His hand was broken. The next morning, Haugsrud fired Blood, Cobb, and Kiesling, although he hired them back that same afternoon. He needed them for the game.

There was the game against the Providence Steamrollers that was a clear example of home-field advantage. The Eskimos could do nothing right, and the Steamrollers could do nothing wrong—at least in the eyes of the hometown refs. By halftime, the Eskimos felt like they had been fighting hand-to-hand, while the other team had been firing heavy artillery. They'd been punched, kicked, clawed, and bitten. Nevers designed a play that put an end to the entire game. At the snap of the ball, the Eskimos went after the referees and the Steamrollers, putting just about all of them out of commission. All three officials were prostrate on the ground, one feebly blowing on his whistle, groaning that time had run out and the game was over. The Eskimos walked off the field, lucky to end up with a scoreless tie.

By 1927, the Eskimos had fallen to next to last in the league standings with just one win and eight losses. The following year, the Eskimos name was gone from the league schedule, never to appear again.

In 1928, John ended up going to the Pottsville Maroons, where he did yeoman's duty on a team that ended the season with just two wins and eight losses. It wasn't the Maroons' best season. In 1925, while Johnny Blood had done battle with Ironwood and Milwaukee, the Maroons had laid claim to the league championship with a 10–2 record. But it was not to be. There was a near-riot in Pottsville when the Maroons were denied that championship, following a calamitous series of events. By the end of November, 1925, the Maroons boasted a 9–2 record and the Chicago Cardinals were 9–1–1. The two teams met at Comiskey Park on December 6, and the Maroons dominated, winning, 21-7. The Cardinals' Chris O'Brien realized that he could schedule a few easy games and improve his year-end win–loss percentage. In hastily arranged matches, the Cardinals beat the nearby Badgers and the Hammond Indiana Pros, ending with an 11-2-1 record.

The Maroons themselves also managed one more game, beating the Notre Dame All-Stars and the Four Horsemen, 9-7, giving them a 10–2 record. Unfortunately, the game was played in the territory of the Frankford Yellow Jackets, and league president Joe Carr suspended the Maroons, fined them $500, and pulled the franchise from Pottsville. Pottsville made it back into the NFL in 1926 and finished third behind the Yellow Jackets and Bears. Meanwhile, the Cardinals tumbled to tenth place. It may have been poetic justice, but some say you can still start a fight in that Pennsylvania mining town if you bring up the year the Maroons were cheated out of the league title.

By 1929, the Maroons were out of the league once and for all and John was looking to take his football skills to another venue. Johnny Blood would become one of the Packers. Football in Green Bay went back to 1895 when a Chicago native named Fred Hulbert arrived with a love for the game and (at least according to a local reporter) the town's first actual pigskin. That fall, he organized some guys from both sides of the Fox River into a couple of football teams and they went at it.

Football in Green Bay began with a flourish in the "Gay Nineties." This first championship team featured Fred Hulbert (third row, far left) who'd brought the sport to Titletown in 1895. Also present was Tom Skenandore (second row, fourth from left), the first professional football player in Green Bay history. Photograph obtained from and used with the permission of Eldon Cleveland.

The first game ever seen in Green Bay was played on Saturday, September 21, at old Washington Park at the east end of Walnut Street. The following day, the *Green Bay Sunday Gazette* reported that "Football has received its introduction to Green Bay and henceforth the 'gridiron field' will be the mecca of the amusement-loving public until snow flies."

A month earlier, the paper had made a prescient prediction:

> It is safe to say that once the game is introduced it will be one of the most popular amusements ever seen in Green Bay. It is predicted that the first game of football played in Green Bay will be more largely attended than a ball game, and that each succeeding game will bring out a crowd.

Thenceforth, football action of the town team variety was a foregone conclusion. And so the Packers were born into a hotbed of football action in 1919. In 1920, they left their town-team opponents behind and joined the American Professional Football Association to do battle on the national stage.

Curly Lambeau was one of the city's first celebrated high school football stars. He took to the forward pass like a bee to honeysuckle. Because the pass was still a relatively new weapon, most opposing elevens were ill-equipped to defend against it and Lambeau rode the pass to early glory—starting with his stint at East High School from 1913 to 1917.

His first choice for college football was the University of Wisconsin, in Madison. But when freshman football was canceled due to a lack of players, he returned to Green Bay. In the autumn of 1918, he tried it again, this time at Notre Dame. There he joined the ranks of pass-oriented Knute Rockne, and his own early propensity for aerial display was reinforced. Lambeau did football battle for the Fighting Irish that fall, but fell ill at the end of the season and returned to Green Bay, never to rejoin the Notre Dame huddle.

In August of 1919, he was elected captain of the Packers and resumed his winning football ways. Lambeau would coach and manage the team until 1949. Unfortunately, the Packers were crushing the rest of the town teams in Wisconsin and Upper Michigan and it was becoming a little bit boring. Like so many other successful town teams across the nation, the Packers were going to have to rise above the local fray and compete nationally. In the process, the roster featured fewer and fewer of the local boys.

The Packers actually fared pretty well in the APFA–NFL once they joined in 1921. Through the 1928 season, they consistently pushed the upper echelon of teams in the league in any given year, always finishing in the top half of the standings.

Preparing for the 1929 season, Lambeau made some of his boldest moves, junking half of his roster in favor of better players. He had always believed in tweaking his lineup a little, but this time he cleaned house and began signing some high-powered free agents in a serious push for a championship.

Curly Lambeau only put in a semester under Knute Rockne at Notre Dame, but he honed his love for the forward pass in the process. His panache would take the Packers from town team to NFL champion. Photograph obtained from and used with permission of Stiller-Lefebvre collection.

He picked the bones of the defunct New York Yankees and got future Hall of Famer Mike Michalske. He also dug into the Giants roster and got Cal Hubbard. They joined previous acquisitions Boob Darling, Red Dunn, Verne Lewellen, and Lavvie Dilweg.

Johnny Blood had been on Lambeau's radar for quite awhile. Lambeau always had his ear to the ground for regional talent, and John's growing football acumen bore notice. John had been penciled in after the Milwaukee Badgers' loss to the Packers in 1925. In 1928, as a Maroon, he'd had an outstanding game against the Packers. He ran for one touchdown, caught a pass for another, and threw for a third. After that, Lambeau had to have Blood in his huddle. One day the following summer, John wrote to Lambeau from New Richmond, offering his football services. Lambeau was back in touch immediately, asking John to catch a train eastward so the two could sign a contract.

The increased use of the forward pass did much to change the face of football. Back in the dark days of the line smash, emphasis had been on the biggest guys a team could locate, though the big guys of that day would look small by today's standards. But the pass demanded fleet-footed backs who could operate on both ends of the play, as well as run the ball to spread out the defense, thereby setting it up for the pass. These utility backs were typically placed in the most strategic position in the single wing, handling the ball on every play. It was all the better if a team had a handful of these guys and could rotate them in and out of the lineup. The Packers' 1929 roster boasted thirteen backs out of twenty-eight men. Of these, Johnny Blood was among the most capable. He was surely one of the most colorful.

Over the years, Lambeau would deal with both sides of the Johnny Blood coin. On one hand, he had a tremendous contributor, a player who could easily turn a game around. On the other, he had a constant nightmare dealing with John's off-field antics. Obviously, the legend of Johnny Blood—already shaped from his time traveling with the Eskimos and other teams—wasn't limited to his great plays. It included his quirky, fun-loving episodes, as well. In Green Bay, John would pile on a lot more of these anecdotes.

According to Packers historian Lee Remmel, the story of John's signing a contract itself rises to the level of legend. "Dear John," said Remmel, quoting Lambeau's letter in which he offered John his initial terms, "I'll give you a hundred dollars a game or a hundred and ten if you won't drink from Wednesday until after the game."

John's reply came in a letter a few days later. "I'll take the hundred," he responded.

Eventually, the two of them would settle on $110, with John still being able to drink on Wednesday. (Whether or not he ever actually stopped after Wednesday has always been a matter of conjecture.)

According to author and Packers Executive Committee member John Torinus, Lambeau eventually assigned tackle Mike Michalske to room with John to keep an eye on the coach's rogue talent. If Michalske failed, went the story, he would be fined $250 himself—hardly pocket change at the end of 1929. After a game in Boston, Michalske got Blood to the train station, but John changed his mind and decided he'd like to stay behind and check out Bean Town. Michalske saw $250 about to slip away with Blood. So he cracked his teammate on the jaw and dragged him onto the train unconscious, delivering him to Lambeau in his sleeping compartment.

Over the long haul, the tradeoff for Lambeau was certainly worth it. While Lambeau, the coach, might not have appreciated Johnny Blood's penchant for the party life, Lambeau, the manager, knew that the off-field antics and on-field heroics combined to bring paying spectators to the game. The resulting cash flow kept the football machine moving. In turn, the cash flow for Johnny Blood kept his party train moving.

Time to Catch Another Train. John stood next to Curly Lambeau in this photograph of the Packers team about to leave for a game on a gridiron in an opposing city. Photograph obtained from and used with permission of the Green Bay Packers Hall of Fame.

John always understood the tenuous nature of his relationship with Lambeau, telling Richard Whittingham, "I got along pretty well with Curly, for a while anyway. . . . For the first three or four years, he put up with me and my antics. I think I was one of the few who could get the best of him, he had a hard time keeping up with me."

Chapter 5

Johnny Blood and the Packers: A Marriage Made Somewhere Outside of Heaven (1929–1932)

In Green Bay, I was intoxicated with the freedom. I was on a plane of emotional enjoyment. Consciousness of the enjoyment of the life I was leading. The first month I was in Green Bay, I got a job at the Northland Hotel (that was the big hotel there) and I had a music box and I had some wax and spread it on the floor and there was action all the time. Now, too much hearing makes me nervous, but then the more noise the better it was. I had no more thought of the future. Sufficient unto the day is the evil thereof. Let the morrow take care of itself.

— John V. McNally

The joining of Johnny Blood with the Green Bay Packers was a near-perfect union. Green Bay had been a football town since 1895, and sports fans there had taken to the game in a big way. The 5,000-seat City Stadium was built behind Green Bay East High School in 1925, primarily as a venue for the Packers, though they would share it with the school at their own convenience. By 1929, it was considered one of the better stadiums in the NFL, especially noted for the quality of its playing surface.

On top of that, Green Bay (thanks, in part, to the adjoining township of Preble) had quite a reputation as a party town among visiting players from other NFL ports of call. Teams would sometimes stay in Green Bay for a three-day soiree, during which they would eventually squeeze in a football game. Otherwise, it was a roving party from one speakeasy to the next, punctuated by a couple of stops at the whorehouse for good measure. The Duluth Eskimos themselves had gotten into a squabble with the police after they had busted down the door of one house of ill repute where the madam had decided the "Iron Men from the North" might be too much for her girls. And that was before Johnny Blood had joined the team.

It was into this mix that Johnny Blood would arrive, by freight train in the dead of night, as a Packers player in 1929. By then, Blood had earned a lofty reputation throughout the league. He was hailed as a broken-field runner who could negotiate his way through random traffic. He could throw the ball with decent accuracy, as well as punt. In a day when defense was the emphasis, punting was considered an offensive weapon if it could pin the other team deep in its own territory. As a defender, he was known as a hawk against the pass and a tenacious tackler.

Above all, he could make the impossible catch. By 1929, he was one of the premier pass-catching backs in the NFL. And he did it all with a certain flair that seemed to make the men drool and the ladies swoon. By this time, John had grown into an extremely handsome man of twenty-five. He was in his physical prime. The Packers roster listed him as a back, at 6' and 190 pounds. It was the combination of his good looks, his football skills, and his natural sense of the dramatic that made Blood such a draw at the gate. It was clear to everyone who watched him that football was just a game—one he was very good at—and, really, so was life. He was known to loaf and clown around when his team was up by a few scores, and to produce the miraculous when time was waning and the impossible needed doing.

Early on, Curly Lambeau earned a reputation as a talent scout. By 1929, he'd successfully turned a powerful town team into a contender on the national stage. Green Bay locals were no longer welcome in the huddle unless they'd acquired some football reputation at a college or on another NFL roster. Because of Blood's Wisconsin roots and because Lambeau had seen and heard of his football prowess, Lambeau was set on getting Blood into the Packers fold for what would prove to be a championship drive. As team manager, Lambeau also knew that guys like Blood helped teams turn a profit. Even in the game's earliest days, money made the whole football wheel turn. By 1929, City Stadium could accommodate turnouts of 13,000 fans, if the team could draw them in.

The area around present-day Green Bay East High School had seen football action since the first game in the city in September, 1895. This is a picture of old City Stadium, north of the school, which served as home of the Packers through the 1956 season. Photograph obtained from and used with permission of Stiller-Lefebvre Collection.

Blood was assigned jersey number 24. His time on the rosters of his previous teams had been a dress rehearsal. Now, he would deliver, game after game, on center stage, eventually being advertised in every city where the Packers played as the man capable of turning any game around at any moment. As such, he would become larger than life, one of the era's super-stars, the drawing card that brought paying fans out to the benefit of the Packers, the home team, and the league. In the process, the stories already in the hopper would be joined by countless others—whether they were true, false or a combination thereof.

"Green Bay was definitely the place for me," John would tell Ralph Hickok many years later. "My destiny, maybe." He added:

I loved the place and, I have to say, the place, the people, loved me. If you play for the Packers, the people in Green Bay know you better than they know their own brothers. And they care more about what you do. I imagine that's not so good if the team isn't going well, but I was lucky to be there during those great years.

One thing about Curly was that his teams always went first class. We traveled on the best trains, stayed at the best hotels. In Green Bay, we stayed at the Astor…. The YWCA was right across from the Astor, and we usually ate there. You could get a terrific meal for seventy-five cents.

And the fall weather in Green Bay was beautiful. A lot of the time, of course, we had nothing to do—and just to do nothing was marvelous, in Green Bay.

Johnny Blood at a Packers practice. He had a reputation for loafing when the team was well in the lead and pulling out the proverbial rabbit when it was all on the line. Don Hutson would one day say that 'no one could change the direction of a game like Johnny Blood.' Photograph obtained from and used with permission of Stiller-Lefebvre collection.

Lambeau's 1929 crew was star-studded. On the roster were twenty-eight men, the largest Packers roster ever, allowing Lambeau to substitute at will. Thirteen were listed as backs—players able to handle the ball on every play, be it a punt, pass, or run. Such capable field generals as Red Dunn, Red Smith, and Verne Lewellen were already in the mix, now joined by the likes of Johnny Blood. It would be Lambeau's last year as an active player, though he saw little time in the lineup. What was the point? He'd had his day, and he'd assembled a team of superstars who could do the job for and without him. Eventually, ten of these twenty-eight players would find a spot in the Packers Hall of Fame. Four of them would someday have a representative bust in the Pro Football Hall of Fame.

Three of John's 1929 teammates really impressed him, he told Hickok: Red Dunn, who could "throw the ball as well as anybody at the time"; Verne Lewellen, who could punt the ball "deep and very high, so there was just never any chance for a return"; and Lavvie Dilweg, who was "a tremendous competitor." John cited the Dunn–Dilweg connection as the reason for the Packers' passing success during the late 1920s.

In 1929, Curly Lambeau led the Packers to the team's first league championship. There were two more to follow—and almost a fourth. Photograph obatined from and used by permission of the Green Bay Packers Hall of Fame.

The season opened with a 14-0 exhibition victory over the Portsmouth Spartans. Then it was five straight league contests at City Stadium—against the Dayton Triangles, Chicago Bears, Chicago Cardinals, Frankford Yellow Jackets, and Minneapolis Red Jackets. They were all wins, but Lambeau's football machine was just getting oiled up. By the end of these five games, the team had scored 79 points and allowed only 6.

Now, the Packers turned into a road team for eight games. The league figured it was best to get the home games for teams in small northern towns out of the way early and then cater to the crowds in their larger member cities. Despite playing its last eight games on the road, Lambeau's team would prove its mettle, winning twelve contests, losing none, and finishing with one scoreless draw against the tough Yellow Jackets.

The first contest was a 7-6 win over the Chicago Cardinals. The following week, they would meet the Minneapolis Red Jackets. During this middle stretch of the season, injuries were especially devastating. Lewellen, Jug Earp, and Cal Hubbard were all hobbled, but Lambeau's bench depth demonstrated his wisdom. In the Minneapolis game, Blood scored an important TD and the Packers escaped 16-6. In the next game, against the Bears, John took over punting duties and hauled in two key passes on the team's first touchdown drive. Minutes later, Dunn suffered a separated shoulder and the Packers' lead passer was sidelined. Still, they managed a 14-0 win.

Then the Packers met up again with the Cardinals and John's old Duluth Eskimos buddy, Ernie Nevers. Dunn and Lewellen were still hurting. John intercepted two of Nevers' passes, one of them leading to a Packers touchdown. In the fourth quarter, the Packers set up for a field goal, Blood holding for Bo Molenda. But the fake was in, and John tossed the pigskin to Dilweg for a second touchdown. The Packers walked off the field 12-0 victors.

Green Bay had been playing cat and mouse with the New York Giants all season long. The Giants, who joined the league in 1925, had been a consistent championship contender each year thereafter. In 1927, they'd won it all, finishing just ahead of the Packers. In 1928, both teams had slid back some, finishing 6th and 4th, respectively. A showdown was in order.

More likely thanks to big-city attitude than to superior talent, the morning line favored the Giants. And so it was that the Packers from little Green Bay took to the Polo Grounds in front of more than 30,000 spectators on Sunday, November 24, against the mighty New York Giants. "This was the first time that I really got the feeling that I was in the big leagues," John told Hickok. "The New York papers devoted a lot of space to pre-game publicity, which we'd never seen before. And it was really something to get out there in front of all those people."

Fortune was with the Packers. Since so many of his players had been on the disabled list, Lambeau had rotated quality backups into the starting lineup—giving them lots of game experience. Meanwhile, his starters had mended. They were all ready for the Giants, who themselves had no intention of being pushed over.

On the first drive of the game, John scooped up a fumble on the Giants 38. Nine plays later, the Packers scored a TD. In the third quarter, Giants quarterback Benny Friedman hit wingman Tony Plansky for a score, however, Jug Earp tipped the extra point and the score stood at 7-6, Packers. Early in the fourth quarter, the Giants had finally gotten on track. Friedman hit end Ray Flaherty for what looked to be a sure score. But Johnny Blood raced upfield and dragged Flaherty to the turf at the Packers' 10 yard-line. On the next play, Friedman was picked off in the end zone.

On the next set of downs, Blood tore off an 11-yard run before the Packers bogged down. They went into punt formation with Lewellen back to boot the ball. Instead, he tossed it to Blood who had slipped past the line for a 26-yard pickup and the Packers were back in business at the Giants' 35. By the end of the game, the Giants had had it. Bo Molenda put the ball over for a second TD. Next, it was Blood's turn—scoring from five yards out, yelling to his teammates, "Let's make 'em like it!" The Packers left the Giants grumbling about a 20-6 beating.

From the party that followed came one of the great Johnny Blood stories. The victory over the Giants had caused some of the Packers to sense the need for a celebration. John was one of the party proponents. Things were going well. Perhaps too well. Boxer Primo Carnera was in attendance. The party was just hitting stride when, at about 2:30 a.m., a terrible shortage was discovered. No, not alcohol—there was plenty of that. It was ice. There was hardly any left.

John was more than a clutch hitter, especially when it came to something this important. He gazed out the window and saw an ice wagon eighteen stories down delivering early-morning ice to the various saloons along Eighth Avenue. He took the elevator down to the lobby, ran through the lobby out into the street, catching up with the ice wagon. He bought a 140-pound block.

He slung the ice onto his shoulder and headed back to the party. It wasn't easy and it wasn't pretty. The ice was cold, slippery, and wet. But a determined Johnny Blood got that ice back to the hotel room bathtub, and the party continued from there.

In essence, by their win over the Giants, the Packers had clinched their first NFL championship. Next up, they faced the Yellow Jackets for the second time in the season. To train for the Frankford game, the Packers took up residence in Atlantic City. The game was set for

Thanksgiving Day. John turned 26 the day before the game and, of course, another party was in order. On game day, the Packers could not muster much offense, perhaps due to some aching heads, and they left town with a disappointing scoreless tie.

The Packers had two more games to play, but they were really mere formalities. Against the Providence Steamrollers (a team he remembered well from the dirtiest game he ever played as a Duluth Eskimo), John chalked up two TDs and the Packers steamrolled the Providence team, 25-0. Next up were the Chicago Bears.

The Bears had been in the league since the beginning, though they'd enlisted as the Decatur Staleys back in 1920. They'd always played a tough brand of ball and had actually won the most games that year, though they placed second to the Akron Pros in year-end standings thanks to the league's use of a percentage system in which ties were not counted. Akron had ended with an 8–0–3 (1.000) record, and the Staleys were 10–1–1 (.909). Since then, the Staleys/Bears had placed 1st, 2nd, 2nd, 2nd, 7th, 2nd, 3rd, and 5th, between 1921 and 1928.

Because of the geographic proximity and the David-Goliath relationship between the two cities, the Bears' and Packers' rivalry was a natural one. The animosity started the first time the two teams saw battle in Chicago on Sunday, November 27, 1921, a 20-0 loss for the Packers. Green Bay had a silver-tongued sports reporter—one George Whitney "Cal" Calhoun—who loved to fan the flames of the rivalry with spicy words meant to antagonize the Bears, as well as any scribe in the Windy City who might choose to engage in some literary sparring.

But in 1929, there were few Chicagoland takers for Calhoun's cajolings. The Packers were on the home stretch of a championship season, and the Bears were just one game away from cleaning out their lockers. Because their last victory would come against the Bears, the ensuing championship would taste even sweeter. The Packers triumphed, ending their season with a 25-0 win. They walked off Wrigley Field that Sunday afternoon as world champions.

The town of Green Bay erupted. The party started the minute word reached Green Bay by telegram of the team's victory. The fact that the team stayed in Chicago overnight only whetted the town's appetite for a proper welcome-home celebration. The next day was bedlam. The *Press-Gazette* reported that the team would be arriving at the Chicago & North Western depot at 8:30 p.m., Monday. It was basically an invitation to Packers fans and all others to throw caution to the winds, check their sanity at the door, and turn out for the kind of homecoming party the town hadn't seen since the end of World War I.

On the train itself, the party had already begun. The national champions were downing celebratory drinks and pouring liquor over one another. Blood was cruising up and down the length of the train, snapping a wet towel at all of his teammates, especially Lavvie Dilweg, the fierce competitor. Dilweg lunged at Blood, who jumped out of the way. Now, Dilweg was furious. He tore after Blood with vengeance on his mind. Blood ran through the train, toward the caboose, with Dilweg hot on his heels. Eventually, Blood ran out of train and ended up on the rear platform of the caboose.

"Now I've got you," Dilweg said, as he opened the door.

"No, you don't," said Blood, as he hopped onto the railing and pulled himself up on top of the car. The train was moving full speed.

It's been said that Blood ran the entire length of the train, right up to the locomotive, where he dropped in on some mighty surprised engineers. That is not true. After all, the prudent thing to do was just what John did do. As he told Hickok,

> I went forward about seven or eight cars, just far enough to get past the Packers' car, and then I came down. I went forward, through the cars, all the way to the front. Then, when we stopped in Green Bay, I got out, ran up to the locomotive, climbed in next to the engineer, and let everybody think I'd made the whole trip on top of the train.

It was an illusion of which Harry Houdini would have been proud. As far as Dilweg's revenge goes, no further report was ever forthcoming. (The myth—that John ran the entire length of the train atop the cars and hopped in by the engineers—was either one Johnny Blood fabricated himself or one that he never chose to straighten out until his interview with Hickok.)

About five miles south of Green Bay, fans had already lined the track, waving red flares to signal a welcome to their heroes. In Green Bay itself, bedlam was in full swing. "All Green Bay welcomed the victorious Packers football squad last night," began Calhoun's newspaper account on Tuesday morning. "And what a welcome it was!" The story went on:

> No warriors returning victorious from a great battle ever received an ovation such as was accorded the Green Bay players when they came back to the city they represented in winning the National professional football championship.
>
> There have been great celebrations here before, but never was there one that equaled that of last evening. The others seemed like a family picnic in comparison to the welcome tendered the football heroes by the crowd of 20,000 persons.
>
> Thousands of persons were everywhere, lining the streets, on tops of roofs and boxcars, in windows hoping to get a glimpse of the players. It was impossible to get close to the Northwestern railroad station at 8 o'clock, a half hour before the train bearing the team arrived.
>
> When the train pulled in at 8:30 o'clock between rows of flaming fuses, thousands who were fortunate enough to get close to the station let out a mighty cheer. It mattered little to them that they were jammed together like bits of sand on a desert, for weren't they among the privileged few who were first to see the champions?
>
> The size of the crowd amazed those in charge of arrangements. None of them had any idea that so many persons would brave the cold to greet the team. But they did. It was a great show of civic pride and indicates that Green Bay's community spirit is of the best....
>
> Traffic was at a standstill for blocks. Every street leading to the station was plugged solid with automobiles, unable to move because of the congestion.
>
> Screeching sirens, bellowing whistles on locomotives and in industrial plants, tooting automobile horns mingled with the cheers as the train pulled slowly into the station. The crowd was so thick that the train was forced to proceed at slow speed with a

brakeman going ahead with an escort of policemen and Battery B guards to clear the path.

When the train came to a standstill, it was all the police and guards could do to clear the way for the players. They finally got the team aboard special busses and, with the American Legion band and Battery B leading the procession, a parade started slowly west on Dousman St. to Broadway, where it turned south.

On both sides of every street along the line of march thousands of persons stood, waving and cheering as the players passed. The parade went south on Broadway to Walnut, turned east to Washington, back north on the city's main street and last on Main to Adams, back to Walnut again, then over to the city hall.

At city hall, Mayor John Diener greeted the team with a speech. Diener also extended to them "the 'freedom of the city for 24 hours,' something that never before has been done for a group of men." Little did Diener know that some of these very men had already enjoyed the freedom of the city, albeit unofficially, on more than one 24-hour occasion.

Dr. W. W. Kelly, team president, and Lambeau were asked to speak, as were several players, though most declined. Johnny Blood did take the platform and said later, "Boy, it was great, and it gave me a thrill to see all those people and to know that they came down to the station just to welcome us home." Finally, the city council passed a resolution thanking the Packers for bringing the city its first national championship of any variety.

Then, a timeout was called. The party would resume the following evening at the Beaumont Hotel. There, each team member would receive a watch and a $220 bonus. The team and a crowd of 400 supporters then broke bread and heard even more speeches, which were actually broadcast live over WHBY radio. Again, Kelly spoke, then Lambeau, who got the evening's loudest round of applause. Lambeau was celebratory. But he also prepped the team and its supporters for the following season:

> It is going to take a lot of hard work, energy and the loyal support of all fans to give Green Bay another championship team next year. Other teams that won the championship always finished in the second division the following year, but we are going to do our

best to break the precedent and if the fans are behind us we think we can do it.

It was quite a promise and quite a task. Lambeau had misspoken slightly in his assessment of the challenge. Back-to-back championships had been won before. The Canton Bulldogs had done it in 1922 and 1923. If history recognizes the Cleveland Bulldogs as a refurbished, relocated Canton team, they were actually the first NFL aggregation to three-peat as champs. The league had also seen several teams—the Bears, the Giants and the Yellow Jackets—consistently among the upper echelon. But no team still in business in 1929 had established itself as a dynasty over the league's first decade of existence, so Lambeau's apprehension was understandable.

While it wasn't intended to be, the banquet's keynote speech was probably Johnny Blood's. Drawing on his experience as a lad reciting "Gunga Din" at Hagan's Opera House he followed teammates Earpe, Lewellen, Dilweg, and Dunn to the podium. After the requisite opening "thank yous" to the members of the football corporation and the fans, he said, "I am especially grateful for the check." He continued, "I'm in the greatest town in the world, and I'm glad to be here—in Green Bay, the home of the perpetual fatted calf."

John's reference to the fatted calf couldn't have been more augural. He'd been New Richmond's prodigal son for some time now and would remain so for the rest of his days. But what he couldn't have known at the glorious end of the 1929 season was that Green Bay would also get into a habit of bidding him farewell and then feasting and celebrating with him upon his return— especially celebrating. The significance of John's speech was conveyed to his hometown newspaper, the *News*, by a New Richmond transplant, George E. Klak, who'd witnessed the championship celebration at the train station as well as the banquet. "New Richmond, no doubt, is vitally interested in the victory of the Packers, for one of its outstanding performers is none other than your very own John Blood (John McNally)," wrote Klak.

In Green Bay, the *Press-Gazette* put it this way:

> Johnny Blood, the "vagabond halfback," almost stole the show with an extemporaneous speech. . . . He recounted his 4 previous years in professional football, saying he had played in most of the

cities of the United States and "starved in many of them," and that this championship healed all the wounds incurred in the beatings he had taken during the previous years.

The season was over, a glorious one by anyone's standards. John would close out his personal business in Green Bay before heading home to New Richmond in a first-class railroad passenger car for the Christmas holidays. He was a triumphant hero. Now that he was gone and generating a name for himself elsewhere, his hometown had taken serious note of him. On Christmas Day, the *News* ran a piece entitled "'John Blood' is Placed on Second All-American Team." "John McNally ("John Blood"), this city," it read, "who this year played a great game of professional football with the Green Bay Packers, is placed at right halfback on the 2d All-American professional football team by C. [sic] W. Calhoun of the Green Bay *Press-Gazette.*" It quoted Calhoun as follows:

> An army of capable backs cavorted on the pro gridiron this fall. . . . Blood of Green Bay, is a "play boy," but on the gridiron, he struts his stuff like the big leaguer that he is. On Green Bay's eastern trip, the St. Thomas [sic] product was very much in the limelight.

Like most of the scribes of his day, Calhoun was all about punch and not so much about fact. Facts were wonderful things, as long as they didn't get in the way of hyperbole. The fact that John had never gone to St. Thomas was a flyspeck of detail; the rest was the truth.

John would have a wonderful off-season to rest up before going back at it as a member of the 1930 Packers team. That winter, he ventured back to the West Coast to renew his acquaintances. As New Richmond's snow melted into the Mississippi that March and April, John was indeed a boy in spring. The following autumn, his football exploits would become a weekly event for folks in his hometown, as Larron "Pipe" Peterson relayed them in his "Pipe's Sports Column" to *News* subscribers.

If Lambeau had tweaked his team during the previous off-seasons, he did a wholesale housecleaning following the 1929 campaign. There were those who doubted his sanity. After all, he'd struck pay dirt with his current roster, so why change it at all? But Lambeau had explained his rationale in his victory speech at the Beaumont Hotel; it would take a lot of hard work and energy to field a championship team in successive seasons.

Johnny Blood was known as a fleet-footed, broken-field runner who could bust open any game with a shift of his hips. Photograph obtained from and used with permission of the Green Bay Packers Hall of Fame.

To be sure, most of those affected by Lambeau's housecleaning were bit players, and he kept his "A-team" in place. He himself had stepped off the playing field and turned the passing game over to his understudy, Arnie Herber. Herber was a Green Bay boy, a star of the West High School teams of the mid-1920s. He'd played freshman football at the University of Wisconsin and then headed off to Regis College in Colorado. Herber was known to have unusually small hands for a quarterback, and his grip of the football was accordingly unique. But he could throw it a country mile and was very accurate, to boot. In the late 1930s, Herber would toss the ball through a two-foot-square glass pane from sixty yards away for a short film, *Pigskin Champions*, featuring the Packers. And he had to do it twice in a row, the story goes, because the cameraman wasn't ready the first time.

Herber's ascension to the lofty position of Packers quarterback was an interesting one. As a high school kid, he'd been something of a mascot to the team and a favorite of Lambeau's, hanging around, gathering up towels and taking good-natured ribbing from the players. It was during his first season with the team as a player, according to Chuck Johnson, that Herber learned a little bit about the football itself from a couple of veterans—notably Mike Michalske and Johnny Blood. There couldn't have been an odder pair of teachers. Michalske was by the book, while Blood was all about avoiding the book and the rules it contained. Eventually it would become Michalske's task to be sure Blood was present and accounted for when the team train or bus pulled out of the station. Here they were, joined for a little trickery on the greenhorn.

"Rookie," Michalske called to Herber. "I'll bet you can't throw a football 100 yards."

"You're right, Mike," Herber responded. "I guess 80 yards is about my limit."

Blood chimed in. "Mike means that you can't throw the ball 100 yards, including the roll."

Herber thought he had them. "You mean you'll give me the distance the ball bounces after it lands?"

"That's right, kid," said Michalske. "We'll give you the roll. Johnny and I bet you $25 each that you can't throw the ball from one goal line to the other."

"You're on," said Herber, already spending his newfound $50 in his head.

Herber took a running start toward his goal line and heaved the ball into the air toward the other goal line. It was a beautiful toss. When it came down, it came down between the 20- and 15-yard lines at the other end of the field. Herber was sure he had it. But a funny thing happened as the ball hit the ground. It bounced backward and came to a stop at the 25-yard line—a good sight short of the projected 100 yards.

At the end of practice, Michalske and Blood grabbed up their $25 each and Herber walked away knowing that a long forward pass puts the nose of the ball into the ground and it bounces backward, not forward—something the two veterans had known all along. (The chances are good that Michalske put his money in the bank while Blood spent his on a foray that night.)

The Packers defense would not be its old-stonewalling self in 1930, and several games turned into real nail-biters. As a token to their town-team days, the Packers entertained an Oshkosh squad, but turned them away, 46-0. Then, as usual, the Packers had to play most of their home games before making like a traveling circus. All of the first four home games played at City Stadium were victories: 14-0 over the Cardinals, 7-0 over the Bears, 14-7 over the Giants, and 27-12 over the Yellow Jackets. Then the Packers had a road game, against the Minneapolis Red Jackets. It was a 13-0 win for Green Bay.

John's personal heroics over those first few games included a clutch interception against the Bears and a spectacular touchdown catch and run against the Giants. But he sustained a rib injury in a collision with Red Grange in the Bears game and his continued participation in the team's contests was on hold.

The next game was a rubber match against the Red Jackets, this time in Green Bay. Again, the Packers emerged victorious, 19-0. Then it was a good old-fashioned behind-the-woodshed beating of the Portsmouth Spartans, 47-13. The next several games represented the toughest stretch of the season. An improving Bears team was factored in twice and the Giants, Cardinals, and Yellow Jackets were all looking for revenge.

Against the Bears, Blood scored a touchdown on a 48-yard pass from Lewellen and followed that by kicking the extra point to make it 13-6. The Bears scored another TD but missed the extra point, and the Packers left Wrigley Field with another victory over Chicago.

The following week, disaster struck. The Packers weren't very acquainted with losing—they had a 22-game winning streak, reaching back into the 1928 season. Though it was inevitable at some point, the following week's loss against the Cardinals, 13-6, was a tough one. His old Duluth teammate, Ernie Nevers, paid John back with some late-game heroics and the Packers had to settle for a split series with the Chicago teams.

The Giants were not happy when the Packers arrived in Gotham for a Sunday, November 23, nose buster. The week before, the Giants had fallen to the Bears and the Packers had clung precariously onto the league lead. This time, 40,000 people turned out to see the game at the Polo Grounds. They weren't disappointed, as their Giants snuck by the Packers, 13-6. The two teams were now dead even.

Four days later, in a couple of key Thanksgiving Day games, the Packers beat the Yellow Jackets, 25-7, and the Giants lost to the Staten Island Stapletons, 7-6. It was John's twenty-seventh birthday.

Johnny Blood, Green Bay Packer halfback, in his heyday. Photograph obtained from and used with permission of the Green Bay Packers Hall of Fame.

The rest of the season was mostly a matter of hanging onto the goods. The last two games produced a 21-0 loss to the Bears and a 6-6 tie with the Portsmouth Spartans. The Packers ended the season with a 10–3–1 (.769) record, and the Giants closed out at 13–4–0 (.765). But, again, league championships were decided by percentage. The Packers had earned their second title by four-thousandths of a point.

On their way home, the Packers changed trains in Columbus, Ohio. There to greet them was NFL President Joe Carr. "When the smallest city in the league can win the championship two years in a row," he told the team, "it's something to be proud of. And I'm as proud of the Green Bay Packers as any of their fans up there in Wisconsin."

At season's end, another classic Johnny Blood episode would be added to the annals. It went something like this: The Packers had traveled to Memphis to play an exhibition game against a crew of all-stars. That crew included a couple of guys fresh from the Giants' squad. At one point, the Packers used the same play they'd used successfully against the Giants at City Stadium earlier in the season. Red Dunn would fake a throw downfield and then toss the ball behind the line of scrimmage to Blood. In Green Bay, Blood had picked up a neighborhood's worth of ground. But the Giants on the all-star team recognized the play and were about to cream Blood. So he tossed the ball back to Dunn. Dunn, completely unprepared for Blood's ad-lib, was tackled for a loss. Blood wasn't the only player on the Packers team caught laughing as Dunn crawled to his feet. Dunn wasn't laughing.

Over the 1930 season, New Richmond fans of Johnny Blood and the Packers had been kept up to date thanks to the Wednesday and Saturday editions of the *News*. On Wednesday, September 10, they read that John had signed his 1930 contract with the Packers as the *Press-Gazette* commented "very favorably on the ability of a New Richmond boy."

A couple of weeks later, "Pipe" Peterson had hailed "Jack" McNally as "without a doubt the most colorful football player that ever flaunted the Blue and Gold with these great Packers." Since the Packers were set to meet the Red Jackets the following week at Minneapolis' Nicollet Park, Pipe ended by saying, "Well, Jack, we'll be seeing you and the rest of your gang over in Minneapolis."

Then, New Richmond fans learned that a rib injury would likely keep

Blood out of the Minneapolis contest. The paper quoted John's mother as saying he would "likely be out of the game for several weeks, possibly for all season." Hopes were dashed. Though the author ended with "All of which is anything but good news to Jack's host of friends here, who had hoped to see him in action with the Green Bay Packers Sunday." By Saturday, October 25, Pipe was reporting to a relieved New Richmond that Blood would be back on the sidelines for the team's next contest, against the Red Jackets in Green Bay. In mid-November, Pipe gave John sole credit for the win against the Bears.

The folks back home had taken to the Johnny Blood stuff in a big way and, when they could, they'd travel across the state to see their "vagabond halfback." "He never got hurt," remembered Harold Lundell. "It would take a broken leg to keep him out of a game."

On Wednesday, December 17, the *News* plucked an item from the wire services that read:

> With the season over, Green Bay's mighty Packers (professional football team) will scatter all over the country until September 1931. Johnny Blood, the Vagabond Halfback, will return to his home in Minneapolis [sic] for a while and then probably hit the beckoning trail. The Vagabond says he would like to see the pyramids of Egypt and as likely as not he will make his way there.
>
> ("Johnny Blood" you know, is our own John McNally. [added the *News*]).

No accounts of John scaling the pyramids were ever reported. Instead, the winter updates to the New Richmond faithful revolved around some extraneous activities on his part. On Wednesday, December 31, the *News* reported that John had returned by train to Green Bay, where he was going into vaudeville at the Orpheum Theatre with a monologue on the 1930 football season.

In January and March, two articles reported on John's off-season success as a member of the Green Bay Packers' basketball team, which was playing various town teams across the state. John had always loved basketball, and now he was starring on the hardwood floor with his Packers teammates, Mike Michalske, Boob Darling, Wuert Engelmann, Dave Zuidmulder, and Arnie Herber.

If the 1929 and 1930 championships had been tough, a title in 1931 was going to be nearly impossible. There were just too many things to go wrong, and the odds against it were that much higher.

The 1931 season would be Lambeau's big test. During the off-season, he again jettisoned nine veterans that he considered the team's deadwood and brought in thirteen new players. Three exceptional rookies were also added to the roster—Hank Bruder, Roger Grove, and Milt Gantenbein.

The season began in the usual manner, with eight of the team's first nine games at home. This had proven a charm in the previous two seasons, giving the Packers momentum as they boarded the train for the rest of the schedule. That season would feature the return of the stingy Packers defense of 1929. The team came out of the stretch of home games with a perfect record, having tallied 213 points and surrendered a mere 42. Most of those first games were uneven affairs: 26-0 over the Cleveland Indians, 32-6 over the Brooklyn Dodgers, 27-7 over the Giants, 26-7 over the Cardinals, 15-0 over the Yellow Jackets, and 48-20 over the Steamrollers. In their last home offering, they waylaid the Stapletons, 26-0.

In the Cardinals game, John's feats saved the day. The Cards actually led at the half, 7-0. But John made two spectacular touchdown grabs and returned an interception for a third TD. The Packers won, 26-7, and Blood had single-handedly accounted for 18 of those points.

Against the Yellow Jackets, Blood plucked a Herber pass out of the air and scored from 38 yards out, and ran another around the

The Vagabond Halfback

Johnny Blood in action in a Packer uniform. Because of photographic technology at the time, action photos were rare and of poor quality. The nickname "Vagabond Halfback" had already been attached to the nickname "Johnny Blood." Photograph obtained from and used with permission of John Doar.

end for 19 yards. The Packers won, 15-7, and John had racked up 12 of those points.

The only other team of concern for the Packers was the Portsmouth Spartans who had, at one point, won nine straight games. The season ended with the Packers in first place with a 12–2 (.857) record and the Spartans in second place at 11–3 (.786). For the third year in a row, the Packers were champions.

A curious complication muddied the waters at season's end. Somewhere along the way, Lambeau had agreed with Spartans coach George "Potsy" Clark to play a championship game against Portsmouth at the end of the season. Since the Packers had ended up a game better than the Spartans, Lambeau told Clark that he did not intend to play the game, creating a maelstrom of protest in the Ohio town. The Spartans insisted on a game with the Packers on December 13. Joe Carr stepped in, however, pointing out that the game was superfluous since the Spartans had lost one more game than the Packers and were clearly in second place. Even a victory in such a game would only produce a tie, necessitating yet another championship game.

The 1931 season was probably Blood's greatest as a pro. He led the league in touchdowns, scoring 13, and he was named to the first All-Pro team along with three of his teammates—Michalske, Hubbard, and Dilweg, the left side of the Packers line. He led the Packers in scoring by posting a total of 78 points out of the team's 291. The next closest was Lewellen with 36.

New Richmond fans had again been kept up to date on the feats of their homeboy. Pipe Peterson celebrated his exploits in the first Cardinals game in Green Bay, suggesting that if Blood had played more extensively there was no telling "just what the final score would have been." Of John, he wrote, "Blood, which is rather a wicked name for a good Irishman, in case you don't already know it, is none other than Jack McNally, man of plenty whims, adventurer and what a football player."

On Monday evening, December 14, John arrived home by train as a bona fide hero. The next issue of the *News* told the McNallys' neighbors that John would be in town, staying with his mother, through the holidays. It included this suggestion: "He is in for a big hand and a heavy welcome from the highly elated citizens of New Richmond, for having placed the city on the athletic map of the country."

John himself had given the *Minneapolis Tribune* an interview, which appeared in the December 22 issue. He said:

> There is no room for loafers in [the] National Professional Football League. The club owners have had little trouble with their players during the past 2 years with the result that our patrons are treated to high-grade exhibitions. If you ask me, the professional teams play football that comes as near being perfect as humanly possible.

It was speculated that John would leave shortly after the holidays to join up with Ernie Nevers' Chicago Cardinals for two exhibition games against the Notre Dame All-Stars, the first on January 5 in San Francisco and the second on January 15 in Los Angeles.

John was home for the holidays and basking in glory. He had proven himself the clutch hitter he'd always admired in Cincinnatus. He was twenty-eight years old, and the small kid had accomplished something mighty big. As Johnny Blood, his was now a household name across the country and folks often wondered who John McNally was. In New Richmond, he was still John McNally and folks there sometimes wondered who, exactly, Johnny Blood was.

The Lumberjack Band was just part of the Packers homespun color. The band was especially popular when it traveled with the team to Chicago to face the Bears or the Cardinals. Photograph obtained from and used with permission of Stiller-Lefebvre Collection.

Halftime

What Did Football Look Like in
Johnny Blood's Heyday?

Technology was bulldozing the American landscape of the 1920s. The radio, telephone, vacuum cleaner, airplane, and automobile were making life easier and faster. Americans were consuming these innovations like wildfire; 60 percent of their purchases were on credit.

It was an era of short skirts and illegal drinking, of petting parties, rampant stock-market speculation, and the first Hollywood stars. Because of its live-for-today attitude, the era was dubbed the Jazz Age. The chatter of the Thompson machine gun in the hands of a big-city gangster added another title—the Roaring Twenties. The Golden Age of Sports was yet another moniker hung on the period. Any decade with that many aliases had to be hiding something and, when the stock market crashed in October, 1929, some embarrassing truths became obvious. All told, the ten years known as the 1920s were a speeding modern roadster headed for a wall. Into this maelstrom, professional football was born, found its legs, and reached for maturity.

The league began as the American Professional Football Association on September 17, 1920. Fourteen men gathered at a Hupmobile dealership to hammer out a football *association*. They would "raise the standard of professional football in every way possible" and, they hoped, avoid a bidding war for star players.

They intended to personally select the championship team. This was imperative, they felt, because their league was so loosely constructed.

Teams set up their own schedules, and a franchise that whipped a slew of weak teams should not win the laurels over a team that had stumbled once or twice against the very best.

The Packers weren't at that meeting; the Bears and Cardinals were. Curly Lambeau would join in 1921, with help from his employer and the push of football-crazed fans in Green Bay.

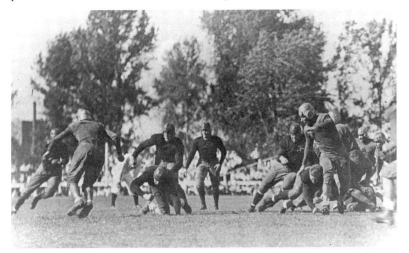

Early Green Bay Packer action against the St. Louis All-Stars, October 7, 1923. The game ended in a scoreless tie. Photograph obtained from and used with permission of the Stiller-Lefebvre Collection.

The Packers had joined an honest-to-God, seat-of-the-pants "national" football association, too flimsy to call itself a league. Like every other team, their schedule would unfold with the season. The only sure game was the one "this coming Sunday" and even it might fall apart thanks to a hundred variables. The *Dope Sheet* kept Packers fans apprised of contests set for the following weekend, as well as those that had disintegrated.

Fans would drive to the ballpark in their black Model T's, one of which was rolling off the assembly line every ten seconds by 1925. The sport they watched there resembled today's spectacle, but with some glaring departures.

The players only dreamed of decent locker-room and shower facilities. In Green Bay, the boys had a clubhouse, which stood prominently on the northeast corner of Walnut and Baird Streets. Before that, they dressed downtown, walked the half-dozen or so blocks to the field before the game, and then dragged themselves back when it was over.

Away games were anyone's guess. In Pottsville, Pennsylvania, the team dressed in a firehouse two blocks from the field. When they played the Staten Island Stapletons, they actually dressed in their hotel rooms and then caught the Staten Island ferry to the stadium, if one wants to use that term.

On the field, goal posts stood on the goal line, so collisions with them were standard fare.

The field didn't have hash marks. A play started on the spot where the last one had ended. If the ball went out of bounds, it was set down one yard in bounds and snapped from there. At that point, a "strong left" or "strong right" formation really meant something. The next play was typically a lateral affair meant to get the ball to the middle of the field, not to gain positive ground.

Teams were working the forward pass into their arsenals, trying to strike an effective balance between running the ball and tossing it downfield. The pass, legalized in 1906 and tweaked in 1912, came with rules that still made it a sticky proposition. An incompletion in the end zone, for instance, gave the other team the ball on the twenty. So much for the improbable fingertip catch in the coffin corner or the Hail Mary. If a team threw the pigskin more than a half dozen times during a game, they were "a passing team."

An aggregation that mastered the aerial game held a wonderful weapon over its opposition; teams that didn't pass didn't defend well against pass plays either. Key to early Packers success was Lambeau's love of throwing. He used the tactic to grind local opposition into the turf, passing more than twenty times in some games.

"Elevens" typically used the single-wing formation, with their best athlete in the "tailback" or halfback position. This guy drove the team's fortunes on the field, handling the ball on every play—run, pass, punt, or dropkick. For the Packers, this spot was filled by Lambeau through 1926 and a handful of men like Red Dunn, Johnny Blood, and Verne Lewellen afterward.

If a team had a squadron of these fleet-footed utility backs and could rotate them in and out of the game, all the better. The Packers roster for 1929, the team's first championship year, boasted thirteen "backs" among twenty-eight men. Their average weight was 190 pounds, with Red Smith, the bruiser back, at 225.

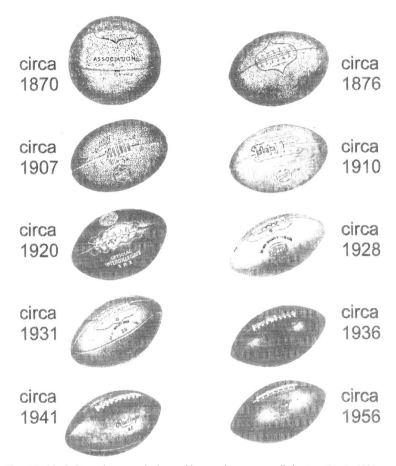

circa 1870

circa 1876

circa 1907

circa 1910

circa 1920

circa 1928

circa 1931

circa 1936

circa 1941

circa 1956

The original football was almost completely round because the game was all about running. By 1906, the pass had been legalized and the ball was getting easier to throw. Pass proponents like Knute Rockne and Curly Lambeau helped keep the ball on its slim course. Photograph obtained from and used with permission of the Green Bay Packers Hall of Fame.

The "quarterback" position had been around since football's earliest days, but it was an anemic sister to today's premier post. The QB stood immediately behind a guard and called the signals, and was little more than a blocking back once the play began. Yet his signals were crucial, as teams rarely huddled before a play, making every play an audible.

Today, we are used to the four-down possession and judge teams by their ability to cover at least ten yards in three downs. The 1920s were quite different. The emphasis was on defense, and it was common to see a team punt on early downs. If they took over inside the 20, they might boot it on first down, pinning the other team in its own territory and hoping to pressure it into a misstep.

Much of the game involved running the ball up the gut. Defenses were happy to oblige by stacking their men tight to the center. With a starting line averaging about 205 pounds, the mass of humanity was not as deadly as it would be today.

Protective gear hadn't advanced much since the 1890s. Jerseys were woolen and notorious for absorbing sweat and rain, ending a game twice as heavy as they had started. Football pants were stiff canvas affairs, with slight padding from felt and fiber. Helmets were leather with nominal padding, feeble enough to be stuffed into a player's back pocket. The players furnished their own gear, except for the jersey.

It wasn't much—the so-called protective padding offered players in Johnny Blood's time. Photograph obtained from and used with permission of the Green Bay Packers Hall of Fame.

For their troubles, including playing on both offense and defense, the average player made around fifteen bucks a game over ten or so contests. If he saved every dollar, the average player would be able to buy a new Model T after two seasons.

The decade hit the wall on "Black Tuesday," October 29, 1929, just two days after the Packers had nipped the Cardinals, 7-6. The Great Depression had arrived and, like the rest of the country, the NFL's freewheeling days were over. Between 1920 to 1929, fifty-four different teams joined the NFL ranks. Some teams were colorful, some were crack football units, and some were nothing more than glorified sandlot teams with the financial backing of someone with both excess wealth and ego. All were hanging on by their fingertips. Only four of those teams, the Chicago Bears, the Arizona Cardinals, the Green Bay Packers, and the New York Giants, exist today.

Fielding a football "aggregation" (a popular term of the day) was like standing up a house of cards. It might look solid one moment and then tumble to the floor the next. If you held it all together, you might build a successful team that would eke out a living, make a name for itself, earn a cadre of loyal fans, and do some actual football battle. But the odds were clearly against it.

It was a nearly identical process in every town that threw its hat into the NFL arena. First, you had to have some "football material"—that is men who could actually play the game. They needed a coach who was up on the latest gridiron strategies, especially formations and actual plays from scrimmage. Until the 1920s, the cutting-edge work along those lines was found in the colleges under coaches like Walter Camp, Amos Alonzo Stagg, Glenn "Pop" Warner, and John W. Heisman. Still, even a coach as far from the football epicenter as Duluth had to stay up to the speed of the college game if he was going to field a winning team; there was always the danger that the coach up the road was installing the latest wing formation or backfield shift.

Second, every team had to have some money up front. Here's where a team manager—a money and promotions man—came into play. Tapping your players to pay for their own equipment was one thing, but asking them to help cover the costs of printing tickets and posters, security, and other non-football expenses got a little sticky. A team with a rich backer— say, an entrepreneur like the Bears' original owner, A. E. Staley—who saw a good team as good advertising had an advantage over a hardscrabble crew pooling their resources. But nine times out of ten, a team was going to have to approach the community for financial support either directly or through dances and bake sales to keep the whole thing afloat. In Green Bay, a group of businessmen known as the "Hungry Five" helped the Packers in this regard. But their nickname came from the fact that their hands were always open and waiting for the next contribution.

Next, you had to have some competition—that is teams who had also managed to pull it all together. In the earliest days of the pro game, this was at best a tentative bargain for the team manager. The accounts of Sunday games falling apart on Saturday evening could fill the guest register at a football funeral home. Regional rivalries were always good for getting the cauldron stirred and the local football fans interested, but the other city had to have an actual team and not just the rumor of one.

Then you needed a good newspaper man. In Green Bay, that was George Whitney Calhoun. "Cal's Comments" wasn't just an exercise in sports commentary, it was a journal of Calhoun's vitriolic rantings and cajolings against teams that thought they might be good enough to play the Packers. Cal was the snake-oil salesman and Packers football was his miracle offering. He was the advance man coming into town ahead of the circus.

Every town with a football team wanted a guy like Cal to stir up the local sentiment because paying spectators—lots of them—were the gas that made the whole thing fly. What if they played a game and nobody showed up? Without filling the stands or coming as close to it as you could, the players, team organization, coach, manager, up-front financial backing, and sportswriters meant nothing. This is why sports writers of the era like Arthur Daley, George Strickler, and Oliver Kuechle were worth the weight of their words in gold.

Every town that had a team had a loud-mouthed cheerleader. George Whitney "Cal" Calhoun of the *Press-Gazette* started his hyperbole with the exploits of Curly Lambeau, and hit full stride embellishing the legend of Johnny Blood. Photograph obtained from and used with permission of Stiller-Lefebvre collection.

The problem of a paying audience is precisely why the NFL found itself at a crossroads when the stock market crashed in the autumn of 1929. The average Joe on whom the whole house of cards depended, out of work and afraid of the future, soon found that he could not afford the cost of the ticket. The Packers dropped the price of their tickets in 1932, to encourage attendance. The cheap seats were just 50 cents. But the practice of sneaking into the game for free became more prominent than ever. There'd always been a certain charm to crawling through the fence near the outhouse wall or making a rush at the gate when the policeman could only stop one or two freeloaders, letting the rest get by. But during the Depression, sneaking in took a sinister turn. Many local papers lamented the mooching fan as a person guilty of killing the very football team he was so interested in watching play. It was an interesting paradox, though hardly a comfortable one—here was Joe with lots of time on his hands to watch football, but no money to buy a ticket.

NFL membership had begun with fourteen teams. By 1921 that number had shot up to twenty-one franchises. Throughout the early part of the decade, membership always stood at or just under twenty teams. But the economic downswing of the late twenties had already whittled the number to ten by 1928. By 1932, just eight teams managed to pull it all together and fight for NFL championship honors. The number would stay at ten or fewer well into the 1940s. Those franchises that did survive had one thing in common —except for tiny Green Bay, they were all located in major metropolitan areas where the fan base was substantial. In Green Bay, dedication to the team was the only thing that kept the Packers from the same scrap heap that held such former powerhouses as the Canton Bulldogs, Rock Island Independents, Pottsville Maroons, Providence Steamrollers, and Duluth Eskimos.

The NFL would lose thirteen more franchises over that dark stretch; some teams foolishly joined the fray during the thirties only to whimper and disappear to the pages of NFL history. Professional football would, however, weather the storm of the Great Depression.

The league's light flickered again during World War II while many of its able-bodied players did their duty overseas. But following that conflict, pro football flourished and grew into what, today, is truly American's pastime and passion.

Following the war, the league took strides to move into its modern era. The sport's overseers had always walked a fine line between the excitement and danger of the game—they were, after all, two sides of the same coin. It was the balance between its roughneck character and "science," as T. P. Silverwood, an early proponent of the game in Green Bay, called it, that had fascinated football's earliest fans.

Keeping the thrill in the game while promoting player safety had always been the goal, and every aspect of the game was touched by it. Changes after the forties—from moving the goal posts to increasing the number of officials to regulating allowable tackling and blocking contact between players—were all attempts to "open up" the game and reduce the number of injuries to players. Helmets went from being optional leather caps to high-tech marvels, and an entire discipline of sports medicine evolved to keep players healthy and in the game. The raw violence of the sport began to abate, but pro football also gained a respectability that made it more acceptable to the mass audience it was attracting.

In the very first days of "King Football" back in the late nineteenth century, the college game had reigned supreme while the pro game was a small-time concern with a reputation like that of a carnival side show. By the 1930s, however, the NFL had started a slow eclipse of the sport as it was being played at the nation's institutions of higher learning. By the late 1940s, the college game had pretty much been relegated to a subservient role, with collegiate programs becoming de facto farm teams providing an endless supply of talent for the professional draft.

At least three attempts were made to form a rival league named the American Football League. The final one was successful enough to garner a merger of sorts with the NFL, creating a football spectacular known as the Super Bowl. By 1970, the two leagues had become one, resulting in a twenty-eight team organization.

Perhaps the biggest influence on what the sport would become, however, was its ongoing love affair with the new forms of mass media that grew up along with pro football. By the 1930s, fans could listen to games broadcast live on radio and watch filmed highlights at their local movie theatres. The color and action of the game made it a natural for the medium that would change football most—television. The sport had seen its introduction on the small screen as early as 1939, when a game between the Brooklyn Dodgers and Philadelphia Eagles was broadcast to about 1,000 television sets in New York City. The money that the NFL and its teams made from television contracts suddenly made the sport a big business, influencing every aspect of the game; and the exposure gave football heroes the kind of cultural impact previously reserved for movie actors and pop stars. By John McNally's death in 1985, eighteen Super Bowls had been played before international television audiences numbering in the tens of millions, fifty college drafts had taken place, and a Louis Harris poll showed that football was followed by 59 percent of Americans, compared with 54 percent who followed baseball. Football had truly become American's real pastime.

So what elements of the gridiron game survive from Johnny Blood's heyday? The love of the game and football fundamentals are about all—though that's quite a lot, really. While the frills around the edge have been tweaked and tweaked again, the basic truths of football have remained rather steady.

This year, millions will watch the games and the debate will rage about the balance between the running game and the passing game, just as it did in the days when Curly Lambeau opened up the running game by spreading defenses that had to respect his double threat in the passing game. Fans and sports commentators will hand the accolades to those who have blocked, tackled, run, passed, kicked, and caught the ball best. Some commentator will dust off the old maxim, "Today's game will be won in the trenches," one more time. There, where the brutes on offense clash with the brutes on defense, the game will be played out once more and a victor will emerge.

Despite being massaged ever since the 1876 Massasoit Convention, the game will remain true to its roots, the roots that Johnny Blood and his teammates and opponents so much enjoyed. That's its beauty.

Chapter 6

The Legend Grows
(1932–1936)

The modern passion for exposure! How greatly it is in evidence on the stage, the street, in art and literature. Everything from physiques to souls are frankly presented to the general gaze. The only prerequisite is the price of admission.

— John V. McNally

As a young man at St. John's University, John McNally had pondered the elements of success as well as its aftermath. The Jazz Age was an era of improvisation and experimentation. The country was watching itself in total amazement. Hollywood was presenting glamorous movie stars like Rudolph Valentino, Douglas Fairbanks, Sr., Mary Pickford, and Clara Bow who, for the first time, became national celebrities—physiques and souls "presented to the general gaze."

Many citizens had shown an open willingness to break the law following the passage of the Volstead Act in 1919, which prohibited the consumption of alcohol. The Roaring Twenties were a moving party, a roving whirl of life on the edge, looking for a place to land. On Black Tuesday, October 29, 1929, the decade ran face-first into a wall and collapsed to the ground like so much bluster. The result was inevitable: a serious hangover that would be felt for the better part of the next decade.

Through the 1920s John had grown to be a man, though hardly

following the manual for the average man. His McNally upbringing in that huge Queen Anne on the corner of West Second and Montana had produced someone who knew the rules, but chose to follow them on his own terms. He'd rejected ordinary and easy paths that had opened before him— a business career at the roller mill, a post in his uncle's law office, even eventual ownership of the *Minneapolis Tribune*. Instead, he'd adopted a persona, Johnny Blood, that allowed him the opportunity to dart between the real and the abstract at will—a perpetual boy in spring. A sportswriter of the time tagged him a "Peter Pan who would never shed his eternal youth."

The National Football League had followed a similar, freewheeling course in striking its own profile. Throughout the twenties, its very existence was often as unpredictable as a gangster Model T, screaming around a city street corner on two wheels, tommy guns blazing. Fifty-four teams would jump in and out of the league between 1920 and 1929. Only eight of those would last into 1930, four of which would be gone by 1932. The Depression rang the death knell on countless teams across the nation, yet the fans' demand for the diversion of football action continued to burn red hot. The only problem was that the fans couldn't afford to buy tickets. Still, on the national stage, some teams did manage to balance it all, if only for a few years.

In 1932, John was in his physical prime. A self-professed "late bloomer" nearing 29 years of age, he stood an earnest 6' tall and weighed in at 190 pounds. His team, the Green Bay Packers, was never on solid financial footing during the thirties. But by passing the hat at the games and around town, they managed to stay afloat. Of course, a big part of that was Curly Lambeau's managing to field a winning organization. They'd just pulled off three consecutive championships.

John's return to Green Bay after a joyous summer in New Richmond was not the glamorous reunion one might imagine. He didn't come riding into town in a brand new car, a freshly pressed suit on his frame. No, he hopped a freight train, having spent all the money he'd earned working over the summer at the mill. "I spent it as fast as I got it," he said. It was vintage Johnny Blood.

At the time, the trip between Green Bay and New Richmond involved two different railroads—the Soo Line, which ran to western Wisconsin, and the Chicago & North Western, which ran as far as Amherst Junction. There, a passenger had to transfer. The problem was, the two trains weren't always in synch. So, with the few coins he had left, John wired the stationmaster at Amherst Junction and asked him to hold the Green Bay train "for a passenger."

With no money left for an actual ticket, John climbed into the blind baggage compartment as the train pulled out of the New Richmond station and headed east. It was slightly better than the freight cars he'd chosen in his youth. At Amherst Junction, John hopped down off the Soo train and ran across the field between the tracks into the blind baggage compartment of the Chicago & North Western train. A few minutes later, after seeing no actual passenger materialize, the Green Bay train pulled out. John's ruse had worked, or so he thought. He was hunkered down in his spot, when suddenly, the door to the baggage car opened behind him. It was one of the trainmen.

"Aren't you Johnny Blood?" he asked.

"That's right," John replied.

"Are you the passenger who sent the telegram?" the trainman asked John.

"That's right, too," he said.

The trainman looked at John in disbelief. After all, the man in front of him was a well-paid, famous football player. "Well, this is the first time we ever held a train for a hobo."

John was invited into the baggage car and treated to a cup of coffee and some of the trainman's lunch. John also borrowed his razor.

When Oliver Kuechle of the *Milwaukee Sentinel* learned of the story, he said he would write it up and call John the "Hobo Halfback." When Lambeau heard of this, he insisted that none of his players be referred to in print as a hobo. In response, Kuechle used the tag "Vagabond Halfback" which had been bandied about on the wire services as early as 1930. Kuechle's use of the nickname, attached to an actual event, assured its place in the legend of Johnny Blood. For his part, Kuechle would get credit for hanging the moniker on John, but it wasn't his to begin with, the name of its originator disappearing from the byline. Kuechle, however, deserves the credit for realizing its resonance. John said he liked "Vagabond Halfback" better himself, since it had "a little more class."

In Green Bay, the Packers were all the rage. If winning three straight NFL titles was something to crow about, should the possibility of a fourth even be discussed? If the Packers could bring home the trophy again in 1932, they'd have surely built a pigskin dynasty.

As a nod to a struggling economy, the Packers lowered ticket prices in 1932. Box seats were lowered from $25 to $20. Reserved seats dropped from $15 to $10, and the rest of the seating dropped by 50 cents a ticket to $1.50, $1.25, and $1.00. End-zone bleacher seats and standing-room-only spots were set at 50 cents, a price almost anyone could afford. All told, it was a bargain to watch the national champions do their thing at City Stadium.

The Depression had drained the league to just eight teams, and Green Bay remained the smallest member city. New York had three teams: the Giants, the Brooklyn Dodgers, and the Staten Island Stapletons. Chicago had two: the Bears and the Cardinals. The Boston Braves and the Portsmouth Spartans rounded out the rest of the league.

Lambeau had done his usual off-season roster juggling while keeping his nucleus intact. Lavvie Dilweg, Jug Earp, Cal Hubbard, Verne Lewellen, Mike Michalske, Hurdis McCrary, Bo Molenda, Tom Nash, and Claude Perry had been on all three championship teams, as had John. However, Red Dunn was not to return, having left the huddle to take the head-coaching job at Marquette, his alma mater.

Nate Barrager, Hank Bruder, Rudy Comstock, Wuert Engelmann, Paul Fitzgibbons, Milt Gantenbein, Roger Grove, Arnie Herber, Harry O'Boyle, and Dick Stahlman had all joined the squad at various points during the championship run. For 1932, Lambeau plugged the remaining holes with seven recruits, the most noteworthy of these being bruising fullback Clarke Hinkle of Bucknell.

The Packers started the season off the right way, with a 15-7 swamping of the Cardinals in a rainstorm at City Stadium; it marked the twenty-seventh straight home win for the Green Bay boys. The following week, the Giants marched into town and promptly marched back out, 13-0 losers. Next up was a Portsmouth Spartans team and another monsoon. The Spartans were undefeated coming into the contest but left with a black eye and a 15-10 defeat. Hinkle proved his value in the game with a sixty-six-yard punt and a touchdown scamper. The Packers were in first place with a 4–0–0 tally.

Green Bay's next game was against the Bears, who were hibernating after three straight ties. It was almost a fourth except that Packer Tom Nash blocked a punt out the back of the Bears' end zone for a safety and a two-point victory.

(Left) Joseph "Red" Dunn was one of the game's first field generals. He played in 58 games for the Packers between 1927 and 1931. Photograph obtained from and used with permission of the Green Bay Packers Hall of Fame.

(Right) Robert "Cal" Hubbard was a tough guy on the field and a straight-talker who was often critical of his coach, Curly Lambeau. Photograph obtained from and used with permission of the Green Bay Packers Hall of Fame.

Next up was a showdown with the Dodgers, who had been nipping at the heels of the Packers since the season's start. The Packers dodged a bullet, and the Brooklyn crew ended up losing, 13-0. Packers fans hadn't witnessed a home loss in thirty contests! The final home game of the '32 season was tagged "Coach Lambeau Day," and the Packers did him proud by pummeling the Stapletons, 26-0. Arnie Herber was the star of the day, making many fans forget all about Red Dunn. He threw two TD passes, ran in an interception for another score, stole one other pass, and punted the ball sixty-nine yards twice. It could have been Arnie Herber Day.

It was the end of October, and the Packers' usual early-season home stand was done. Now, they would take their 7–0 record on the road. If they enjoyed their usual traveling success, they'd return home on December 11 as four-time world champs. The road trip would start in Chicago against their perennial nemesis, the Cardinals. From there, the trip was scheduled to take a sharp left turn toward the East Coast, then veer through Ohio on the way back to Chicago.

Against the Cardinals, Johnny Blood had his own field day, scoring two TDs on passes from Herber and setting the Packers up for a third with a 32-yard circus catch from Lewellen. Blood would continue his winning ways the following week, joining Lewellen and Roger Grove in scoring a touchdown each on the way to a 21-0 shellacking of the Boston Braves.

Next up were the Giants, who'd succumbed pretty easily back on October 2. A couple of days prior to the game, John connected with old buddy Ernie Nevers for a couple of drinks. Nevers had retired from active duty in the NFL, but was assembling an all-star crew for some exhibition play. Nevers told John that he'd been approached about playing a contest in Hawaii, but he hadn't pursued the possibility.

On game day, it was pouring rain at the Polo Grounds and the field had turned to muck. By game's end, the Packers had experienced their first loss of the season, 6-0. It was a sign of things to come. The *New York Times* described one of John's scampers in the contest as a "beautiful run by fast-stepping Johnny Blood."

The Packers were ensconced in first place, but the Bears (thanks mostly to five tie games) and the Spartans were still in the thick of it.

The Packers redeemed themselves the following two Sundays. Still in Gotham, they fought the Dodgers to a 7-0 victory and whipped the Stapletons, 21-3. They had two games left. On the surface, at least, things seemed to be turning their way.

In Portsmouth on Sunday, December 4, however, the wheels would come off. It was cold. Herber, the league's leading passer, struggled mightily, throwing three interceptions and completing just one pass in a dozen attempts. The Spartans also partially blocked two Packers punts and led 13-0 at the half. They added six more unanswered points in the second half, and the Packers undressed in the locker room following the game with two losses hanging over their heads. The Spartans' regular season was over, however, and with only one loss they were sitting on a better winning percentage than the Packers.

It was after that game, en route to the Packers' hotel, that John decided to put to use the information he'd garnered from Nevers a few weeks prior. He sent off a telegram to the sports editor of a Honolulu newspaper, a feeler as to whether anyone would be interested in bringing the Packers to Hawaii for some exhibition football. In a few hours, John had his reply. He was put in touch with one Scotty Shuman, and negotiations were underway for two games. He ran the idea past Lambeau, who said it would take $9,000 plus expenses for the whole thing to happen. Blood wired back, telling Shuman that it would take $10,000 plus a cut of the gate receipts. The deal was done.

One game remained—against the Bears, who were hanging onto a bizarre 6–1–6 record. Since ties were not factored into the equation, the Bears were actually also holding a better percentage than the Packers. Snow fell on Chicago for three straight days prior to the game. It snowed all during the game itself. On top of that, several Packers were down with colds or the flu. Worse, the Bears game was another disaster for Herber, who at one point dropped the ball at the Bears' one-yard line and could do little else the rest of the day. Meanwhile, the Bears put up nine points in front of their fans and sent the Packers back home on a very quiet train.

John told Ralph Hickok that the loss to Chicago had surprised him, especially after the team's excellent Friday practice. "I never saw such a workout. Everybody was running hard, catching the ball, hollering, and four of us were kicking the bejesus out of it. It was one of those emotional things that happen. It was really spectacular, we were really on an emotional high. Then, on Sunday, we were flat."

With identical percentages, the Bears and Spartans met for an indoor playoff game at Chicago Stadium, which the Bears won, pulling down the league title in the process. The Packers fell to second place with the Spartans just behind them. For the first time since 1928, the NFL pennant was hanging in a town other than Green Bay. Had later rules been in place, the Packers would have been enjoying their fourth straight title. They'd also posted more victories (10) than had the Bears (7) and the Spartans (6). Some called it highway robbery.

John tied with Hank Bruder as the team's leading scorer, though his output had dropped from 76 points in 1931 to 24 in 1932. None of his touchdowns had come through rushing. At season's end, he was given honorable mention on the NFL's All-Star team.

Although there was no league title in 1932, the Packers were given a great post-season excursion—starting with the two exhibition games in Hawaii. It was nearly enough to soften the blow. Lambeau and seventeen of his players were to travel to the sunny island. John had made quite an impression on rookie Clarke Hinkle, as Hinkle later related to sportswriter Myron Cope:

> My rookie year we played twenty-two games, fourteen of them league games and eight exhibitions, and we were still playing in February, almost March, and the reason we were was Johnny Blood. Now there's a guy! Let me tell you about him.
>
> He was a rangy halfback, about six-two and 190, and he had great speed. When he was about thirty-five and Don Hutson was about twenty-four, he raced Hutson a hundred yards. Hutson could outrun the wind, but he beat Johnny in that race by only a step. Johnny was the kind of guy who would read Shakespeare, Chaucer, and all those kind of people, although when he was drinking he would read filthy dime novels.
>
> Johnny's life was probably even more glamorous off the field than on. After a game he'd buy up whorehouses. He purchased them and closed them up. Yes, he'd close them up so he could stay with those girls all by himself. I doubt if he had relations with any of them, but that's just the way he was. He liked an unusual conversation. He just liked to do things like that. So during my rookie season he was corresponding with some people in Honolulu, and one day he came to us and said, "Do you want to play a few postseason exhibition games in Honolulu? All you got to do is say yes, and I'll arrange it."
>
> Nobody took him seriously. Lambeau said, "Okay, John. I'll let you handle it. You make all the arrangements."
>
> Well, darned if Johnny didn't get us all lined up for Honolulu.

And so it was that Blood, Lambeau, and a horde of their closest friends and allies headed west for some football and related frolicking. On December 13, they pulled out of the Chicago & North Western station on Green Bay's near-west side, headed for LA. Problem was, Johnny Blood wasn't on the train. In his mind, the levity of a year-end football frolic had already taken hold.

It seems that John's girlfriend at the time was a nightclub singer in Green Bay. They were driving her car to the station but were running a bit late. John was pounding the gas pedal to compensate. That caught the attention of one of Green Bay's finest, and the next thing John knew he was explaining his situation to the policeman. After finding out who he was and where he was going, the cop let them go, however, they were now hopelessly late. And indeed, at the appointed time, the train began pulling out of the station. At the first intersection, there was a problem. A car was parked across the tracks, and the train had to come to a stop. It was McNally, who kissed his girlfriend, grabbed his bags, and climbed aboard.

"I could see Lambeau wasn't happy," John told Hickok, "but he didn't say anything. Nobody did. I was pretty popular because I'd arranged the Hawaii trip." In Tucson, John's popularity spiked even higher when an acquaintance of his got on the train with some moonshine. "From then on," he told Hickok, "we had a merry trip."

Because of Prohibition, most of the players had never had a legal drink in their lives. That hadn't prevented most of them from *illegal* drinking, however. But once their steamship was three miles off the California coast, drinking was plenty legal. "We were traveling second class," John told Hickok, "but they gave us the run of the ship. And the Packers were pretty well known, with those three championships, so we had no trouble at all making acquaintances. We had a ball."

Blood had agreed to keep the public posted on their progress in the pages of the *Green Bay Press-Gazette*. His byline, "The Vagabond Halfback" began appearing the following week. He wrote, "When Green Bay and Wisconsin football fans read this, the Packers will be on the briny deep, bound for the Hawaiian Islands, the home of the hula dancer."

He also updated Green Bay fans on his teammates, suggesting that Arnie Herber had been "barred from all future card games. He's too lucky.

Mike Michalske is lonesome and is already pining for old Green Bay."

Furthermore, Blood promised that, upon arrival in Honolulu, the Packers "will immediately begin working out for the contest with the University of Hawaii Christmas Day. The Packers will be 'strictly business' until this game and there will be no sightseeing until after Christmas." It was a claim that stretched the credulity of fans in Green Bay.

The Packers played a couple of games against hybrid teams of college and semi-pro players, won them both and headed back home—after the requisite "sightseeing." But one more legend had to be etched in the Johnny Blood file first.

It seemed that his reputation as a skilled drinker had preceded him. John had done pretty well in the first game on the islands, so the Honolulu footballers came up with a strategy for the second contest that was meant to take Blood out of the game. They determined to pit John against one of their players at a luau the night before the two teams lined up against one another. John shakily recalled the story later:

> They put me up against their toughest drinker, a big tackle for their team. We drank their national drink, Okolehau, and we drank into the night and morning. I got about an hour's sleep, but I showed up at the game. Their big tackle didn't. I remember I was not feeling too terrific as the game started. Then a shower burst through the sun and I got my refresher and then went on to score a couple of touchdowns.

On the return trip to the mainland, Blood added one more chapter. Hinkle remembered it this way:

> We were having a good time on the boat, when suddenly we couldn't find Blood. So Milt Gantenbein, who was my roommate at the time—Milt and I walked out on the main deck and went back toward the stern. The sea was a little rough, and that ship was pitching. But we walked back there toward the stern, and then we turned white. We froze.
>
> Johnny Blood was outside the safety railing, on the extreme stern end of that ship. He was hanging onto the flagpole. There he was, in the middle of that pitch-black night, with the ship

pitching, and he was swinging around that flagpole. He didn't even know he was in any danger.

He'd been drinking that Okolehau, the native drink made from pineapple juice or tea roots or something. Hell of a drink, I'll tell you. Anyway, we eased out there and got him out of there, but if he'd have dropped off that stern, nobody would have ever found him. And that's just one of the things he did.

Back on terra firma, Blood proceeded to pass out in the office of San Francisco Mayor Angelo Rossi's office, thanks again to too much imbibing on the boat. John explained this to Myron Cope, saying, "Alcohol, you see, hangs onto me. I don't sober up real fast. It's a family characteristic—I have plenty of recuperative power, but alcohol doesn't fall out of me. It hangs onto me."

While in California, John got to spend an evening with Red Grange, who'd put him on the disabled list for a couple of weeks back in 1930. Grange described John and another piece of the legend to Cope:

Talk about swingers, what about Johnny Blood? One year, I played a couple of post-season games for Green Bay and roomed with Blood. What a guy! I remember a couple of girls wanted Johnny to sign a program, and he said, "I'll do better than that. I'll sign it in blood." He cut his wrist with a knife and signed that program in blood, and had to have about four stitches taken in the wrist.

He was a loveable guy, a very learned guy, and one whale of a football player. A long-legged guy who could kill you every way. Run, punt, pass, catch passes, a great football player. He used to drive Curly Lambeau crazy. We were staying in Los Angeles, and Johnny and I had a hotel room next to Coach Lambeau. Curly was in the corner room. Johnny knew that Curly had a case of whiskey in his room, so when Curly went out, Johnny climbed out on the ledge, which was on the ninth floor and must have been about a foot wide, and he walked along that ledge for about twenty feet and got through Curly's window and took a couple of bottles and came back. I don't think Curly ever did learn who stole his whiskey.

Over the next few weeks, the Packers played more exhibition games—between parties—against semi-pro and college alumni teams. Like the two Hawaiian games, one of these was broadcast live on Green Bay's WHBY radio.

John's procurement of a couple of bottles of whiskey from Curly Lambeau's room wasn't the only "high-wire act" he performed outside the hotel rooms during this time, either—at least according to early Packer writer Chuck Johnson who recorded the following story:

> The Packers were in Los Angeles one time for an exhibition, and Blood locked himself out when he left his key in his hotel room. It was after curfew when Blood returned from a night on the town and Lambeau was sitting in the lobby, but Blood remembered that he had left the window open. Blood's room was on the fifth floor. He climbed up the outside fire escape and entered a teammate's room that was on the sixth floor, but across an eight-foot court from Blood's room. Then, in a driving rainstorm, Blood leaped from one ledge and across the court to the other, climbed to the window of his own room and went to bed.

In California, John wasn't far from Catalina Island where he'd put in a few winters between pro football seasons. At one point on Catalina, he told Hickok, he'd worked twenty-four hours a day—eight hours at a brick factory, eight hours as a bouncer and stick man at a casino, and "eight hours honeymooning a redhead." John was reflecting on his time on Catalina with a little nostalgia, and wanted to return to the island immediately. Unfortunately, a familiar problem reared its ugly head: he didn't have the money. John set about hitting up Lambeau for some cash. Of course, he'd been on shaky terms with Lambeau over the past few weeks, starting with the car-on-the-tracks incident and continuing over the moonshine and Okolehao bouts. Of course, he'd also arranged the whole Hawaiian trip and pulled in an extra grand over Lambeau's request.

John asked him for an advance and was told "No" about as fast as a person could be. Lambeau went up to his hotel room. John thought it over and called Lambeau. Once again, he was told, "No" in no uncertain terms. John went up to Lambeau's room, pounded on the door and asked again.

Lambeau was peeved by Blood's persistence and said, "No" once more, a little more sharply than before.

"For once, I'm going to know exactly where you are," Lambeau told him. "You're going to have to stay right here in this hotel, because I'm not going to give you any money. I don't want you to call again, and I don't want you to knock on this door again."

That seemed to close the subject for Lambeau who went to bed. But the subject certainly wasn't closed for Blood, not by a long shot. He was more determined than ever to get to Catalina. He couldn't call, and he couldn't knock on the door. But he could crawl in a window. The climbing kid from New Richmond sweet-talked a maid into letting him into an open room directly across an airshaft from Lambeau's room. He crawled out of that room's window and stood on the ledge. It was drizzling, John was eight stories up, and he had a twelve-foot standing broad jump to get to the opposite ledge—no problem for the field-day phenom from St. John's.

At that point, Mike Michalske looked up from his room on a lower floor and spotted John.

"Is that you up there, Johnny Blood?"

"It's me, Mike," John answered.

"What are you doing?" was Michalske's second question.

"Curly wants me to discuss our strategy for the game, so I'm going to his room," John answered. And with that, he made his jump.

And, he made it. Perched on the ledge outside Lambeau's room, John hoisted up the window and slid inside. The next thing Lambeau knew, he was wide-awake and staring straight at his right halfback, who was standing before him with a grin and an open hand.

Lambeau was both upset and amazed. "My wallet's in there," he said, pointing to his pants hanging over a chair. "Take all the money you need. Just don't ever do anything like this to me again."

When once asked what he would have done if the window had been closed, John replied, "I would have kicked it in, of course." Twenty years later, John said that Lambeau was able to laugh about the experience. "But he wasn't laughing then."

The next day, John was off on a little diversion to Catalina Island. He was returning to Avalon.

Following the second contest against the University of Southern California All-Stars on February 5, the Packers broke camp and went their separate ways. Michalske and Jug Earpe had already headed back a week earlier. The last person back to Green Bay was Lambeau, who spent some time in California and vicinity "on business," at least in theory. Blood, meanwhile, found his way back to Honolulu where the Okolehao and hula skirts had caught his fancy.

The heartbreaking loss of the 1932 championship put the entire Packer organization into a long-term funk. The 1933 season turned out to be a disappointing embarrassment. The Packers posted a 5–7–1 record—the first losing season in the team's history.

Some wondered whether the team was going to make a successful transition into a changing league. The NFL had broken into Eastern and Western Divisions and adopted a playoff format for determining league championships, but it was a league dominated by big cities. In the Western Division with the Packers were the Bears, Cardinals, Cincinnati Reds, and Portsmouth Spartans. For the first time ever, the Packers had played a home game at Borchert Field in Milwaukee—a concession to the need for more money at the gate that a larger city might produce. There were those who said it was the first sign that Green Bay would lose its franchise and that Milwaukee would be to blame.

Most of the old guard from the championship years seemed to have lost their individual mettle. Instead, names like Goldenberg, Monnett, and Hinkle had replaced Lewellen, McCrary, and Blood. As in years past, the Packers began their season with a nearly straight set of home games and then went on the road. But unlike the championship years, their record at the end of the home stretch was not enough to give them momentum on the road.

They opened with a 7-7 tie against the Boston Redskins, then lost two in a row to the Bears, 7-14, and the Giants, 7-10. They picked up wins against the Spartans, 17-0, and the Pittsburgh Pirates, 47-0. Then they went to Chicago where they tripped against the Bears, 7-10. Their last home game for the season came the following week, a 35-9 victory over the Philadelphia Eagles. The rest of the season they eked out just 3 wins in games that were all on the road.

By the end of the '33 campaign, John had dropped to fourth place on the scoring board—racking up just 19 points to Charles "Buckets" Goldenberg's 42. He'd displayed individual heroics: a 43-yard touchdown catch against the Giants, a 50-yard catch and run for six points against the Bears, a key interception against the Eagles. But due to injuries, including an infected hand and a nagging ankle sprain, he'd played in just nine of the team's thirteen contests.

Lambeau was putting his emphasis on younger players, and the team was struggling as a result. Blood, Comstock, Dilweg, Engelmann, Hubbard, McCrary, Michalske, and Perry all remained from the championship teams, but it was clear that the lamp was dimming. Lambeau himself had been ailing, consulting a doctor after three straight losses in November. The prognosis was a "stomach disorder brought on by nervousness," and he was put on medication and a strict diet.

The Packers were doing poorly on the field, but they were doing just as badly at the bank. The Packer Football Corporation had gone into receivership, and Lambeau was directed to cut expenses, including waiving some players. The Depression was howling at the door, and the team's on-field fortunes weren't staving it off. "The Hungry Five"—a handful of Green Bay businessmen—were now forced to pass the hat around town to save the Packers. They would eventually raise $15,000. But it was only a start in bailing the team out of its financial difficulties.

Toting a 4–4–1 record into New York, the team was set to face the Giants on Sunday, November 26, a day before John's thirtieth birthday. That night, a surprise—John was ready for bed when a call came. It was the wife of a millionaire from the Fox River Valley (whose name has always been fodder for the rumor mill but has never been positively confirmed). She was at the Stork Club and wanted John to join her. John declined the offer, deciding instead to get some needed rest with the game just two days off. It was an amazing display of self-discipline for a guy who was always at the ready for a little adventure.

Then, there came a knock on the door. "And there," John told Hickok, "were these two goddamned nurses. They were Packers fans, they said, and they wanted to meet us. So my roommate and I invited them in and had some drinks sent up." As a matter of fact, John and his roommate had a lot of drinks with the nurses that night. The next day was Saturday, and the Packers were set to practice in the morning. John showed up, hung over.

"Curly gave me kind of a funny look when I came onto the field," John said. "I guess it showed. Then, when I tried a punt, I missed the ball completely and fell flat on my ass. Curly sent me back to the hotel."

At the hotel, after practice, Lambeau told John he was being released from the team.

"I didn't argue," John told Hickok. "I just said, 'Okay, Curly,' and I walked out. I couldn't really argue."

John's firing from the Packers was a signal of something, but what? He was thirty years old and still fit. Yet nagging injuries had started to hamper his availability. Lambeau's official reason for letting him go was listed as "breaking training rules," but Lambeau had enough stress putting a winner on the field, let alone keeping track of his wayward star. On the other hand, there were plenty of people suggesting that Lambeau had sent Blood packing because he upstaged his coach in the fan spotlight.

The idea that John had been let go for breaking training rules prompted some chuckles around town and some genuine complaints. John wasn't the only of Curly's players known for ignoring Lambeau's rules, though he was surely the most celebrated. Then there was the fact that Lambeau himself had a reputation for drinking and womanizing, which he hadn't acquired at St. Francis Xavier Cathedral. Besides, John's anonymous roommate, who'd also partied with the nurses, hadn't been let go, had he?

John took up with a semi-pro outfit in Paterson, New Jersey, for the next few weeks. He needed the money. Meanwhile, the Packers had lost to the Giants and beaten the Eagles. The last game on Green Bay's schedule was against the Bears in Chicago. The NFL had been split into Western and Eastern Divisions for the first time, and the Bears were well in front in the West with a 9–2–1 record. Lambeau got ahold of Blood and asked him to return to the Packers for that last game of the season. Blood agreed, but it didn't matter. The Packers lost a close one, 7-6, and John was never used in the contest.

The fact that he'd technically ended the season as a Packer was good enough for John. But the next few months were a meandering jumble, even for a vagabond halfback.

After the Bears game, he headed to the West Coast to reconnect with one of his San Francisco buddies, Aloysius "Shanty" Malone. Malone owned a San Fran bar, and John was one of his favorite patrons. Blood used a familiar mode of travel to get there, hopping trains. For a few weeks, he worked a pick and shovel on a WPA project outside of Los Angeles to earn some pin money.

John went to work as a bartender for Malone. "Shanty owned several different places through the years," John told Hickok, "and I tended bar for him several different times. His places were all pretty much alike—genteel, in a knock-down, drag-out kind of way."

A longshoremen's strike early in 1934 put John on a boat. "I didn't want to be a scab, necessarily," John said. "By that I mean that I had no interest in helping the boat owners break the strike. But I did want to go to sea.… I signed on as a supposedly able-bodied seaman."

He worked on freight boats, traveling to Yokohama, Hong Kong, Hawaii, the Philippines, Panama, and Cuba. He found himself doing an overnight in jail thanks to "a matter of principle. I don't remember now just what principle it was, but no doubt it was very important to me at the time," he told Hickok.

In Shanghai, he missed his boat by a few minutes and with no girl-friend's car to park in its way, he fell back on some tricks that had worked in the past. He jumped for the boat's railing but missed and ended up in the water. "I landed in a whirlpool, or something," he told Hickok. "The water was just very heavy, and it was almost impossible to swim. Fortunately, some people pulled me out and got me aboard."

John got back to the States in early summer to find out that the Packers had sold him to the Pittsburgh Pirates, who would become the Steelers in 1940.

"I think Curly had rehired me for that last game in 1933 because he realized that I'd be a free agent if I was still fired at the end of the season," he explained to Hickok. "This way, he got some money for me."

Lambeau had a reputation for being something of a conniver, especially when it came to personnel moves. He hadn't been above using some college players in a game in 1921, that almost cost Green Bay its NFL franchise permanently at the league meetings that winter. His veterans often lamented on how difficult it was to negotiate an increase in salary with

Curly. Meanwhile, he was known to sell them suits and insurance on the side (especially in later years) tapping their paychecks for the cost.

Buckets Goldenberg suggested that contract talks with Curly were "like a three-act play." He suggested that Lambeau kept three sets of contracts—one to be sent to the league offices, one for the club records, and a third set that he kept under lock and key in his desk. "That one," said Goldenberg, "was the one he brought out when you asked for more money." Lambeau would badger the player, waiving the contract at the player, suggesting that the contract in his hand was that of Clarke Hinkle or Don Hutson. "Do you think you should get more than they do?" Lambeau would ask the wilting player. "It wasn't until afterward that I found out that those contracts that Curly had locked up so well were phonies," Goldenberg said.

In regards to Johnny Blood, what he'd ostensibly done was bring him back under contract for that last game in order to continue holding his rights and enjoy any profit there might be in trading the wayward halfback. If he'd simply cut John after the "nursing incident," he'd have had to watch John sign on with another team as an unrestricted free agent, owing nothing to the Packers.

So, John ended up in the Steel City for the 1934 season. Pittsburgh, the football team, stunk. They'd entered the NFL's Eastern Division in 1933 and gone 3–6–2 for last place. Throughout the entire league, only the Cardinals had fared worse at 1–9–1. Pittsburgh wanted John for his receiving talents, but they had absolutely no one on the roster that could throw it downfield to him. A pesky ankle injury compounded the problem. The Pirates ended the '34 season a dismal 2–10–0. John wanted out of Pittsburgh and back in at Green Bay. Pittsburgh owner Art Rooney acquiesced and released him from his contract.

Back in Green Bay, the Packers had muddled their way through a 7-6-0 season, putting them in third place behind the Bears and Detroit Lions in the Western Division. The Lions had appeared on the scene that year as a relocated Portsmouth Spartans franchise. Lambeau's annual team tweaking wasn't paying the dividends it had just a few years earlier. Only Dilweg and Michalske remained from the championship teams, and the new guys had yet to hit stride.

However, in 1935, by a matter of minutes, Lambeau scored the big one—a 6' 1" end out of the University of Alabama who would dominate the league for the next decade. His name was Don Hutson.

Hutson had come to the Packers with about an hour to spare. His skills were so highly valued that Lambeau and the owner of the Brooklyn Dodgers, John "Shipwreck" Kelly, got into a bidding war over the Alabama Antelope. The price got up to $175 a game, which was unheard of at the time. Lambeau agreed to the price and sent a contract off to Hutson by airmail. Hutson hadn't heard anything from Kelly for a few days and thought he'd lost interest. He signed Lambeau's contract and returned it. About an hour later, Kelly showed up at Hutson's home. To be fair, Hutson signed an identical contract with Kelly and called Lambeau to tell him of the latest development. Lambeau said it was no problem. He immediately forwarded Hutson's contract to Joe Carr, the NFL president. Lambeau's contract arrived about an hour before Kelly's, and Hutson was a Packer.

Don Hutson was clearly the NFL's first super receiver. Hutson and McNally usually lined up on opposite ends of the line of scrimmage; still, their friendship was enduring. Photograph obtained from and used with permission of the Green Bay Packers Hall of Fame.

Long-time vets like Hubbard, Swede Johnston, and Walt Kiesling bolstered Lambeau's 1935 team. Players like Bruder, Gantenbein, Goldenberg, Herber, Hinkle, and Monnett were coming into their own. It looked like Lambeau had effected the magic one more time. Still, he was without fan favorite Johnny Blood, and he often heard it on the streets of Green Bay. Lifelong fans like Nubs Pigeon and Ray Drossart recalled telling Lambeau repeatedly to "bring back Blood."

After some training camp time outside of Rhinelander, Wisconsin, Lambeau took his show on the road, playing four exhibition games against semi-pro teams from across the state. Blood decided to market himself to his old coach the old-fashioned way—by playing standout football for two of those four teams, the Chippewa Marines and the La Crosse Old Style Lagers. While the Packers handled both of the challenges, 22-0 and 49-0, respectively, Blood impressed Lambeau enough to ink a deal the following week. Shortly afterward, John wired Art Rooney and told him he had a chance to return to the Packers. Rooney was agreeable and released him from his contract with Pittsburgh.

John told Hickok:

> I think Curly rehired me partly because he could see that Hutson and I could be a really devastating combination. I was thirty-one going on thirty-two, now, but I really hadn't slowed down much, if at all—maybe because I was such a late bloomer. . . . But I think another reason was the fans. They'd been pretty upset about Curly getting rid of me, and there were a lot of complaints. The fans really liked me—hell, I'd probably had a drink with every one of them, at one time or another. But that also caused problems with Curly. His ego had really got swollen by this time, he thought he was football in Green Bay, and I think he was kind of jealous of me.
>
> He'd sit me on the bench for no particular reason, and then the fans would start chanting, "We want Blood! We want Blood!" And finally, he'd put me back in. Or we'd be behind, and he'd have to put me in to try to get back into the game. That's one reason I developed a reputation as a clutch player, I think—a lot of time, Curly would only use me when he really needed a big play."

In the first game of the '35 season, neither Blood nor Hutson started and the Packers fell to the Cardinals, 7-6. September 22, in a game against the Bears, however, Hutson demonstrated the genius of his hiring as he hauled in an 83-yard Herber toss and cruised downfield for a TD and a 7-0 Packers win. That put an end to the Bears' three-year dominance over the Packers. On the scoring play, Green Bay unveiled an odd formation, with Hutson split left and Blood flanked to the right. "It was similar to the pro set they use now," John told Hickok. "We used it all the time, with Hutson and me. But this was the first time anybody had seen it."

The ball was snapped to Herber and he dropped back. Blood had drawn most of the Bears' coverage. Hutson faked left and slanted across the middle of the field. Herber landed the pass on stride, and Hutson scored the game's only touchdown. Best of all, it was the game's very first play from scrimmage.

Five weeks later, Hutson sealed the deal when his two-touchdown performance helped kick the Bears again, 17-14. But in both games, Johnny Blood's presence on the other side of the field did much to draw coverage away from Hutson. It would be another quarter century before the Packers would sweep the Bears again.

Blood was knocked out of the Cardinals game on October 13 with a serious concussion. He'd performed one of his circus catches and been smeared by three Chicago defenders. Speculation had him out for the rest of the '35 campaign, but he was back in the lineup three weeks later. In the meanwhile, Hutson carried on without him. In the Lions game on November 11, Blood caught two touchdown passes—one for eighty yards and another for twenty.

By season's end, the Packers had amassed an 8–4–0 record and found themselves in second place in the Western Division behind the Lions, who ended with a 7–3–2 mark. Once again, the NFL's method of counting (actually, *not* counting) ties had cost the Packers a shot at the title. In the East, the Giants had won the thing handily and toed up against the Lions for the championship game, which the Lions won, 26-7.

Johnny Blood began the 1936 season by holding out for more money — a bold move considering his contentious relationship with Lambeau. Still, he understood his importance in the dual passing threat when teamed with

Hutson. "I was getting $150 a game, and Hutson was getting $175," he told Ralph Hickok. "I figured I deserved to get paid as much as he did. Curly didn't see it that way, at first, but he came around after I missed the first three games."

It was the Packers' first-ever contract holdout. John went over Lambeau's head to get the raise, which was no doubt a factor in his release at the season's end. As he told Richard Whittingham, instead of dealing with Lambeau, he approached the Packers' board of directors and said, "I made All-Pro last year and I'm underpaid here." They agreed and gave Lambeau his orders.

The '36 season would be John's last in Green Bay. He would actually lead the team in passes caught—25—with Hutson hauling in 18. His longest catch would be 70 yards, and he would cross the goal line three times for 24 points. He was the team's second-leading scorer behind Hutson. He had 42 rushing attempts for 115 yards. He would also toss the ball 33 times, completing 11 for 164 yards.

It wasn't a bad way for an old man of thirty-three to close out a chapter of his pro football career. And his final season contributed at least a couple more stories to Blood's legend. His first action of the season hadn't come until the fourth game, a 31-2 thrashing of the Boston Redskins. Against the Lions on October 18, Lambeau drew up a quirky game plan, based on the previous year's game in which the Lions had picked off four Green Bay passes and essentially cost the Packers the championship. There would be "absolutely no passing," Lambeau said.

That was fine for awhile, but eventually the Lions stopped looking for the pass and focused their energies on the run. By the second quarter, Hinkle was getting nowhere. Lambeau decided he needed a clutch hitter and sent Blood into the game. "Remember, no passes," he said as he pushed Blood out onto the field. The Packers moved the ball inside the Lions 20, but the Lions jammed Hinkle twice in a row at the line.

Then, Johnny Blood did exactly what Johnny Blood would do—he called a pass play. Blood and Hutson veered outside, taking the majority of defenders with them. Milt Gantenbein broke across the middle and caught Herber's pass for a touchdown. Lambeau was livid. In a heartbeat, Blood was back on the bench. "If we lose this game, you are responsible," Lambeau told Blood. "How could I lose the ballgame sitting on the bench? We're ahead and

I'm out of the game," John remembered thinking to himself.

The Packers held onto the lead, but by the third quarter the champion Lions had closed the gap. It was 10-9, Packers. The City Stadium crowd began its chant. "We want Blood! We want Blood!"

Lambeau caved. "If you call a pass, you're fired," Lambeau cautioned Blood as he sent him back in.

Anyone who knew Blood knew what would happen next. "Fake the handoff to Hinkle and zoom it to me," he told Herber. "I'll be open. Just zoom it."

Hutson and Blood took opposite sides of the field—Hutson left, Blood right. Hutson would likely draw double or triple coverage, John figured, and it was up to him to do the rest. Of course, Hutson had been in the game the whole time and Blood was coming in on a fresh pair of legs. So the Lions focused on him instead. He went downfield with three Lions defenders. Herber faked to Hinkle and then lofted the ball in the direction of Blood and the pack of Lions. It was a total mess—four men straining for the pigskin.

But when it was all said and done, Blood came down with it and fell across the goal line for the touchdown. Lambeau was livid but relieved. The Packers were ahead, 17-15. "I guess I was unemployed for about 55 yards," John would later say.

After a field goal, the Lions were back on top, and Blood did it again. He called a pass to Hutson with just seconds left on the clock. The completion put the ball on the Lions' 18-yard line, and a field goal from there gave the Packers an 18-17 victory.

"After the game," John told Whittingham, "Curly never mentioned the pass. I didn't mention it to him either."

In the next game, Blood caught a touchdown pass and ran for an extra point to help the Packers in a 42-10 whipping of the Pirates. For much of the rest of the season, Blood was an expensive bench warmer as Curly showed him who was boss. The Packers went into their final game, against the Cardinals, needing a tie or a win to clinch the Western Division title. John started the game, but no player could do much on a field with icy spots all over it. The game ended in a 0-0 tie.

But the Blood legend grew by one more story in the game. In the huddle, Blood called a play, "Forty Double X." Now, the Packers had "Forty," and they had a "Forty X"—they were two of their signature plays. But not one player in that huddle had ever run the "Forty Double X."

"What's that?" wingback George Sauer asked.

"Just do what you do on forty," Blood told him. That meant that Hinkle would take the handoff and cut through the hole off the guard position.

Blood took the snap, but faked the handoff to Hinkle, then he faked a reverse to Sauer and followed Sauer around end. "On a good field," John told Hickok, "I would have had a touchdown. But I slipped on the ice and then somebody pushed me out of bounds just across the fifty."

John's sharp mind had designed a new play on the fly, and, in some ways, the double-cross had been on the Cardinals, as well as his teammates.

One game remained for the Packers: the championship game against the Boston Redskins, who'd won the Eastern Division title. The game was played at New York's Polo Grounds on December 13.

John started this game on the bench once again. In fact, he spent the entire first half there. It was well into the third quarter, with the Packers

Here Curly Lambeau preps his team for the 1936 NFL championship game against the Boston Redskins in New York. Often, his "vagabond halfback" would take over at the chalkboard as the team reshaped one of Lambeau's impossible plays into a workable scheme. Photograph obtained from and used with permission of David Zimmerman.

holding onto a slim 7-6 lead when Lambeau sent Blood into the brawl. On his very first play, he put the game out of reach. Referred to by Arthur Daley of the *New York Times* as "Green Bay's 'old man,'" John hauled in a 52-yard pass from Arnie Herber. Blood "never made a move," wrote Daley, "until

Herber had thrown the ball. It was a terrific toss, 65 yards in its flight, but the pigskin wobbled in midair; Blood, swinging left again, had to chop his stride to pull it down." Blood was tackled on the Boston eight-yard line, and a play later Herber hit Hutson for the TD. The game ended 21-6, and the Packers had put another championship trophy on the mantel.

But it was time for John to catch another train, this one out of Green Bay for good. Lambeau decided not to give the vagabond halfback a contract for the 1937 season and a $3,000 offer from Art Rooney to coach and play for the Pirates was hard to pass up. But there was another reason to go. "I just felt I couldn't play for Curly anymore. And I know he was glad to see me go at last. We were both chasing the same woman at the time, and the Pittsburgh job took me out of the picture."

There is some speculation about just who that woman was that both Lambeau and Blood were chasing. The fact is that Lambeau was on his second marriage at the time, to Susan Johnson, an attractive model who had recently competed in a Miss California contest. Lambeau's first marriage, to his high school sweetheart, Marguerite Van Kessel, had fallen apart thanks in large measure to Lambeau's off-season "scouting missions" in Calfornia. According to author David Zimmerman, his name had been linked with actress Myrna Kennedy, as well. So what were the chances that the woman in question was actually the second Mrs. Lambeau—Susan Johnson? Zimmerman states:

> While Lambeau was experiencing success with the Packers during this time, his marriage to Susan was heading in another direction. Susan, only 32, and eleven years younger than Curly, wanted more from her marriage. With each passing year since their wedding in 1935, they spent less time together.

The other possibility is that it was another woman entirely. Lambeau had a reputation among the ladies. He also had one among his players, for moving in on their dates when he saw the opportunity. John's natural intelligence, wit, and charm were certainly formidable and the chances are good that he had the upper hand when it came to head-to-head competition with his coach for a woman's attention.

And there was yet another reason to go—John's regular violation of the rule against drinking the night before a game. Ralph Hickok relayed a story about Tess Doherty, long-time owner of Green Bay's Midtown Tavern, describing a Saturday-night ritual: "Curly would come in here, looking for Johnny. I always told him the same thing—'Curly, he's three times seven, isn't he? Don't worry about him, he's old enough to drink.'"

"I was reckless, they said, on the football field," John would say later, summarizing his Packers days for Whittingham.

> Reckless in a lot of things, I guess. I liked to have a good time back then: women, travel, a little drinking, loved to spend money. I had a lot of experiences. I was very uninhibited, that way all my life, even as a little kid.

John's relationship with Curly Lambeau is an interesting one, one that might have been complex or, maybe, really quite simple. Understanding Curly Lambeau could be a full-time job for a qualified psychiatrist. Understanding Johnny Blood would be an impossible task. Both pursuits have occupied dozens of authors. Larry Names, who began a resurgence of Packers history books with his series *The History of the Green Bay Packers*, offered the following in regards to Lambeau's releasing John under the guise of "breaking training rules" at the end of the 1933 season:

> Was Lambeau jealous of Blood as Johnny claimed in later years? Yes, he was. Curly liked being center stage—alone. He had that much ego. He didn't like sharing the spotlight with anyone; and the older he got, the more attention he demanded. Lambeau singled out Blood because the Vagabond Halfback was more popular than he was that season. Besides that, Blood made the perfect scapegoat for the Packers' losing season—if Lambeau needed one. It would have been easy to blame Blood for his off-the-field shenanigans as being a bad influence on the younger players and for undermining Lambeau's authority.

Zimmerman, who published the very first biography on Curly Lambeau, *The Man Behind the Mystique*, said:

> Lambeau was truly an enigma. His persona was "all in the eyes of the beholder." Regardless of how he was seen by others, the

Lambeau story unfolds like a novel. It has all the ingredients of good fiction: courage, valor, conquest, infidelity, honors, greed, pride, envy, joy, sorrow, shame and redemption. The story of Curly Lambeau is really about a small town boy who rises up along with his hometown to gain national fame only to fall from grace. After years of disgrace and wandering, he returns home to regain his lost fame and dignity.

Zimmerman quoted the inscription next to Earl Louis "Curly" Lambeau's picture in his high school senior yearbook: "When I get through with athletics, I'm going out and conquer the rest of the world."

It is rumored that John's inscription in his high school yearbook read "How sweet in spring it is to be a boy." That was actually a quote from a poem he wrote at St. John's University, but it will suffice. The line certainly reflects his attitude when he was nineteen, the same age as Lambeau when he chose his yearbook quote.

The relationship between Lambeau and Johnny Blood McNally, then, may come down to inscriptions. Lambeau's is about ultimate conquest, victory, and the laurels won when all others have been vanquished. McNally's is about freedom, celebration, and joy. They were bound to clash—the physical conqueror and the unconquerable spirit. In the end, deciding who was the victor (if a victor is needed) might come down to what we value ourselves—the apparent victor or the irrepressible essence.

Tracing the relationship between these two men to practical terms can be done anecdotally. The stories—and there are plenty—mostly revolve around Lambeau, the would-be conqueror, trying to get Blood, the maverick, in line—by slapping him with fines for breaking training rules or releasing him from the team for perceived insurrection.

"Johnny Blood was the most fined man in the NFL," was a familiar refrain from his former teammates. It was rumored that there were even times when, fined once again by Lambeau, Blood actually owed the Packers money until his next paycheck. Lambeau himself once said, "Johnny Blood was the most fined man in pro football. But he never complained, whether it was for $25 or $200. He'd just say, 'I had it coming, Curly,' and pay." But exactly who was the winner there?

Was it the violation of training rules that really irked Lambeau? If, as Names suggests, it was a matter of laying down the law and showing who was boss, then Lambeau may have had cause. But if it was really a matter of putting Blood in his place because he was the fan favorite, then there was a deeper-seated psychic tension at work in Lambeau's actions. Hearing the bleachers echo with "We want Blood!" when Lambeau had relegated the fans' hero to the bench certainly didn't reaffirm Curly's authority or his popularity.

Many of Lambeau's players suggest that when it came to the Xs and Os of football, Lambeau was often in over his head, especially early on. Cal Hubbard was not only a 250-pound behemoth at his tackle position on the line, he was an outspoken student of the game of football. Of Lambeau's own football acumen, he told Ralph Hickok:

> To be frank Curly really didn't know that much about football. After all, he just spent one year at Notre Dame, how much did he learn? Most of us knew more, because we spent more time learning during the four years of college and then, for most of us, some professional experience, too. Hell, sometimes Curly would design a new play, draw it up on the blackboard and we just knew it wouldn't work the way he drew it up. He'd have impossible blocking assignments, or the play would just take too long to develop. The defense would mess it up before it got going. We'd have to tell him that, and one of the veterans would go right up to the blackboard and change it around. Most of the time, Johnny Blood was the spokesman because he was always ready to speak up to Curly.

To Hubbard's description of these scenes, Blood himself added, "Not that I necessarily did the thinking. As Cal said, I was the spokesman. I'd go up and get the chalk, and then we'd all kind of talk about it, a group discussion, and we'd keep working on it until we got it right."

In Curly's defense, Mike Michalske threw in, "I will say that Curly was willing to learn from us. He really learned football from his players, and after a few years I think he knew as much as any coach in the game. He just had to have that learning experience for awhile."

But who was it that had been selected by the group to assume Lambeau's place at the chalkboard? Who was it that found himself up in front of his teammates with the chalk in his hand leading the group discussion? Well, that was none other than Johnny Blood, the natural leader—not elected and given a title, but rather chosen through mutual consent. And standing there, reworking Lambeau's ill-conceived original plan, who was most likely to bear the brunt of Lambeau's chagrin? Why, that was Johnny Blood, too.

So it was no surprise that John became Lambeau's favorite whipping boy, the one of whom he wanted and needed to make an example. After all, how could a vagabond stand in the way of Curly conquering the world? When he fined Blood for a violation of a rule or benched him at the start of a game or fired him, it was a punishment doled out along official lines, and there weren't any fans in the immediate vicinity to mitigate on behalf of their hero.

When it came to the fans, Lambeau also walked a tightrope in regards to his superstar. He could only berate his star back so far before the fans would begin their ranting, "We want Blood!" Fans sometimes told Lambeau right to his face to get Blood back in a Packer uniform. The chanting and cajoling may have irked Lambeau, but he also understood that those voices belonged to paying spectators—well, at least most of them—and paying spectators kept his football machine rolling. Whether Johnny Blood clowned downfield at the end of a pass play when the Packers were up by three touchdowns or made one of his patented impossible catches in traffic for a big gain—it was all the same to the fans. They loved it. And it wasn't just Packers fans either. Lambeau had been upstaged by his star in places like New York, Pittsburgh, Chicago, Hawaii, and California, too.

Despite his embarrassment at the hands of his halfback at the chalkboard and on the sideline, Lambeau still appreciated Blood's intelligence and his football sense. Zimmerman wrote:

> While they had a somewhat adversarial relationship during the years Blood was with the Packers, Lambeau still let him call all the plays on the field. Lambeau would often comment on how he couldn't understand how such an irresponsible character off the field could be such a fine strategist on the field.

Johnny Blood's days as a Packer were numbered in the 1936, even though Green Bay fans couldn't get enough of him. Photograph obtained from and used with permission of the Green Bay Packers Hall of Fame.

That Blood understood their relationship seems pretty clear—he was the philosopher able to view the world and his place in it from a position of self-imposed distance. Lambeau could never have seen it in the abstract, being too devoted to "conquering" to step back. It's why he couldn't understand how John's antics away from the game came from the same place as his skills in the game.

In the end, they were bound to part company, only to be reunited down the road as two of the first men inducted into the Professional Football Hall of Fame. John probably summed it up the best when he told a sportswriter, "Curly didn't completely understand me. But I don't perfectly understand myself."

Chapter 7

Looking for the Coach, the Private, and Reality (1937–1945)

The inferences to be drawn from these instances is that our failures should be but steps on which we rise to the bright particular star to which our wagon is hitched. The lesson to be learned is that we should ever keep a stout heart, faith in ourselves, and a mind alert to apply our hard-won experience to every new problem.

— John V. McNally

Does John V. McNally own a piece of the Pittsburgh Steelers, or does Johnny Blood? The difference is crucial. If in fact, John V. McNally, son of New Richmond, Wisconsin, does—then, the team's present owners had better figure something out because the deal is real. However, if a piece of the team is actually the property of one Johnny Blood, then the controversy is the stuff of legends and nothing to worry about.

For many years, the debate was a source of constant tension between John and Steelers owner Art Rooney. Author Ralph Hickok was on hand at a reception at the Pro Football Hall of Fame as the debate unfolded and the two tossed in their respective points. Here's the story:

In 1937, John was hired to coach and play for the Pittsburgh Pirates. He'd spent one God-awful season there in 1934—as a class receiver waiting downfield for a pitchman. As for the Pirates, it would be three more years before they would become the Steelers and a very long time before they'd see NFL success.

For his pains as both player and coach, John was paid $3,000. For all of his bumps and bruises garnered as a Packers player in 1936, he'd received $2,100 (or $1,800, depending on whom you believed). Johnny Blood had an expensive lifestyle—wine, women, and song did not come cheaply. The extra $900 would prove valuable.

But on top of the salary, he said that Rooney offered him a part of the struggling franchise, which has now won five Super Bowls and placed nineteen men in the Pro Football Hall of Fame. Rooney had been around sports for much of his adult life. He himself had enjoyed some success as a welterweight boxer and a minor league baseball player. Like Curly Lambeau, George Halas, and countless other guys, he formed a semi-pro football team named the Hope-Harveys. By 1933, he'd bought himself and Pittsburgh an NFL franchise at the going rate of $2,500 and borrowed the name "Pirates" from the city's popular baseball team. Halas had seen that same light when naming his club the "Bears"—a close association with the baseball Cubs.

After his first dismal season as a Pirates player–coach in 1937, Blood decided he wanted no further part of it. It was nearly an unbearable load. After all, he described his job as more like coach and player, trainer, and business manager. He told Rooney of his retirement decision. It was then, he said, that Rooney offered him 15 percent ownership of the team if he would stay.

Rooney denied the claim all of his life. "I don't want to argue with John Blood," Rooney stated. "I like him. I think he was a great football player, and I think he could have been a great coach because of his intelligence. Unfortunately, he just wasn't disciplined enough to do it."

Art Rooney was known as a tough-talking Pittsburgh ward boss. John McNally said that Rooney had offered him part ownership in the Pittsburgh Pirates. Photograph obtained from and used with permission of Jim Jameson.

In those words, one cannot find a clear denial to John's claim. But without a piece of paper outlining the deal, there was no evidence to support John's claim, either. "I may have told Johnny he'd have a piece of the team if he did well. I honestly don't remember," Rooney said, closing his part of the discussion. "But I certainly didn't promise him 15 percent of the franchise. If I had promised it, he'd have it. Anybody in Pittsburgh will tell you that."

Blood countered Rooney's assessment of his coaching failures:

> Part of my problem was that I concerned myself too much with the marginal players, trying to make something of them.... It could be that that stemmed from my own background. I was a later bloomer, remember, and maybe I was hoping that those marginal players were later bloomers, too.

One example concerned four players whom John had waived. After cutting them loose, he made calls to other teams in an attempt to find them further employment. He even persuaded Rooney to pay for their way to hook up with the St. Louis Gunners. When they didn't make the Gunners roster either, they wired John back and asked, "Where to now, Coach?"

"Unfortunately," John chuckled, "I didn't have an answer for them. There have been many times in my life when I asked myself, 'Where to now?' and didn't get an answer."

The stories of Blood's tenure as a coach added to the epic of Johnny Blood. Like the stories of his time as a player, they were often three parts truth and two parts fiction—or vise versa. His position of authority as a player–coach hadn't changed McNally's anti-authoritarian ways. Many of his former players and Rooney himself have all been credited with the line, "On most teams, the coach goes out the night before a game looking for his players. On our team, the players went out the night before a game looking for the coach."

However, Rooney spoke to the shaky reliability of most of the Blood stories with a comment to Hickok:

> It may have happened that way. That was a long time ago, and, you know, it's really not important. It's like a lot of stories, it's a good story, but sometimes you embellish a story a little to make it even better. You know there are a lot of Johnny Blood stories like that—some of them aren't true at all, some of them are partly true, most of them have been embellished a little.

There is the story of the missed game, told so often it has all the qualities of a game of Telephone. The fact is, John was not with his team for a game in the 1938 season, but his explanation and the story often told are a world apart. The missing coach suggested that his absence from a game in late 1938 was actually the owner's fault.

There was also a whisper about the time John remained in New York while his team headed back to Steel Town. Two days later, went the story, he showed up at the Giants' offices, disheveled and in need of money. He'd been rolled. "It was tough enough [for McNally] to manage Johnny Blood," wrote John Torinus, "without the added responsibility of a whole team."

John was known to miss team practices, though he always left assistant coach Walt Kiesling with explicit instructions of what he wanted done. He told Hickok that he spent the missed practice time doing research for *Spend Yourself Rich*, a book on economics he wanted to write. "Maybe once every two weeks, I'd get a couple of bottles of milk and hole up in the library, studying," he said.

There was also the story about John putting himself into a game against the Packers as a substitute. Rooney had it that John's own team captain asked the ref whether such a substitution had to be accepted, and the ref said, "no," so the Pittsburgh captain turned him down. Again, John had an entirely different account, which he relayed to Hickok:

> We were playing Green Bay, and we had a lot of people hurt. Lambeau and Red Smith [Packers assistant coach] had been telling everybody I didn't know how to block. I didn't appreciate that. Hell, other players know whether you can block or not, and nobody I every played with said that I couldn't block.
>
> On top of that, the Packers had a Sunday morning meeting at the Northland Hotel the day of the game, and Lambeau had written, "Today, we're out for Blood" on the blackboard. One of my friends on the team told me about it.
>
> Well, we needed a blocking back, so I played 60 minutes at blocking back that day. That put Kiesling in charge of the team from the bench. In the fourth quarter, he figured I must be tired, and we were losing, so he sent a substitute in for me. But I waved the substitute away, because I was the coach. You see, that's how crazy rumors start.

John's results with the Pirates weren't all they might have been. But as a coach, he took over the team with his usual gusto. Their record the previous season had been 6–6–0, and he felt good about his nucleus—especially John Karcis, a solid veteran back; Stuart Smith, a fast receiver; Bill Sortet, a veteran end; Armand Niccolai, a decent kicker; and Max Fiske, a journeyman quarterback.

Johnny Blood still cut a handsome profile against the autumn sky as a player-coach with the Pirates. Unfortunately, the Pirates never fared very well under John. Photograph obtained from and used with permission of John Doar.

But John also inherited a squad that was short on experience and depth. In his first year, he had just fourteen players return from the 1936 season. Thirteen of the thirty-one men who played for him were rookies.

Many of the players were locals, rather than high-quality imports from the various football schools across the country. Six of his players came from nearby Duquesne, two from Pitt, one from Temple, and another from Carnegie Tech.

John's lack of bench strength was his undoing, plain and simple. Coaches like Curly Lambeau had long seen the importance of depth and the resulting ability to substitute freely—especially in the backfield where most of the action was generated. Over the three championship seasons, at least four out of every ten players on Lambeau's roster was a back who could run, throw, catch and, in most cases, kick the ball.

John's 1937 season started off well enough, with victories over the Philadelphia Eagles and the Brooklyn Dodgers. In the Eagles game, John returned a kickoff for a 92-yard TD and hauled in a 44-yard toss from Fiske. Arthur Daley of the *New York Times*, who probably loved the vagabond halfback like no other sportswriter, described John's kickoff return as follows:

> The ball spun through the autumn air and landed in his arms. Johnny took off and never stopped until he'd crossed the opposite goal line a hundred yards away. "That's the way to do it, fellows," said Johnny, dusting off his hands.

The result of the Philadelphia contest was a 21-14 victory, a great start for the player-coach and his team.

In the Brooklyn game, Blood caught consecutive passes of 15, 32, and 6 yards for a touchdown and a 21-0 win. The rest of the season was a downhill tumble. Losses to the Giants, Lions, Bears, Redskins, and Cardinals put the team into a serious slide. As a coach, John tried to evoke the same emotion from his players as he himself possessed. At the practices he did make, he'd have them doing calisthenics, shouting, "Pirates never quit!" It didn't seem to work. His team may not have quit, but they got worn down by the fourth quarter in most contests. They had second-half leads against New York, Detroit, and Washington, but couldn't sustain the effort.

On the field, he continued to impress spectators. He was a one-man wrecking crew in the team's first game against the Redskins, snagging touchdown catches of 43 yards from Fiske and 28 yards from Karcis, and tossing another 55-yarder to Clarence Thompson. Still, the Pirates wore thin toward the end of the game and lost, 34-20.

In a 13-7 defeat by the Cardinals, John was injured and for the next two games did all he could from the sidelines. Another victory over the Eagles, 16-7, helped set things right for one week, but the team fell flat against the Giants, 17-0, the next Sunday. Then, the Pirates edged the Redskins, 21-13, and set their sights on their last game, a return match against the Dodgers. That loss, a 23-0 whipping, put a dark lid on a 4–7–0 season, good enough for third place in the East.

At the end of the '37 season, Blood tendered his resignation, which Rooney chose not to accept. Instead, as John remembered it for Ralph Hickok, that was the point at which Rooney sweetened the offer *verbally* with a 15 percent ownership of the team.

In the off-season, John produced a masterpiece as the team's manager by drafting college phenom Byron "Whizzer" White, who would become not only a great NFL player but also a lifelong friend and supporter of John McNally. The favor would be returned during the 1972 presidential campaign when John spearheaded a drive to draft White, by then a Supreme Court justice, for the Democratic Party nomination. In 1938, however, their relationship would be about football.

White's coming out of the college football ranks was something akin to the emergence of Red Grange or Don Hutson before him. He was a hot commodity after his 1937 season at the University of Colorado, where he'd rushed for over 140 yards per game, scored eight touchdowns from midfield and beyond, completed 21 of 43 passes, and punted for a 42.5-yard average. The Pirates

One of John's best moves as Pirate coach was picking up the contract of future Supreme Court Justice Byron White. The two of them hit it off immediately and remained dear friends throughout their days. Photograph obtained from and used with permission of John Doar.

offered White a two-year contract worth $15,000.

But there was more to it than just money. Like John, White was a smart guy. He'd graduated first in his class and had been elected to Phi Beta Kappa. He also won a Rhodes Scholarship, which John McNally had attempted himself. As far as White was concerned, he was heading off to England to study at Oxford University. That's when Johnny Blood's own shrewd cunning clicked into gear. He checked with the Rhodes Scholarship officials. White could play football and enter Oxford at the next semester. John had also convinced Rooney to double the original contract offer to $15,000 per season.

The 1938 season looked promising. White was being added to a roster that had acquired a season's experience under Blood's sometimes eccentric tutelage. A quick-study, John had now acquired some sense of what it took to "play" in the NFL as a coach and not as a player. And while he was inclined at season's end to catch a train out of town, he was being called on to stay and put himself into something in earnest rather than once more play the dilettante or vagabond.

It wasn't all gravy, however. John tried to orchestrate a trade with the Packers that would put Swede Johnston and Buckets Goldenberg in his huddle, while sending Pittsburgh draft picks Pat McCarty and Ray King to Green Bay. Goldenberg, who'd been John's teammate with the Packers in 1933, 1935, and 1936, nixed the deal, saying he would retire before playing for the Pirates. Blood laughed, replying that Buckets was just jockeying for a "boost in his paycheck." The deal did indeed fall through, however, and Johnston and Goldenberg remained on the Green Bay roster. In fact, Goldenberg would remain there through the 1945 season, eight years after announcing his "retirement." Blood did acquire Walt Bartanen, a tackle, from the Packers in exchange for end Ed Brett.

Blood opened his 1938 training camp outside of Pittsburgh. He had been approached that summer by a 17-year-old John Doar, the son of W. T. Doar, Sr., about serving as a ball boy. The McNallys and Doars went way back. W. T. had shared a room with young John McNally as he established himself as a young New Richmond attorney. W. T. and John's mother, Mary, were second cousins and had always been close. John Doar's mother was John McNally's first-grade teacher, calling him the smartest student she'd ever taught, but even she was leery. "John McNally's life was not the life she wanted for her son," Doar remembered.

The thought of young John Doar under the dubious supervision of Johnny Blood sent tremors though both households, and it seemed that John understood the reservations. "We have to get your parents' permission," he told young Doar. They succeeded, but not without some lingering trepidation. "The story in the family is that mother went to bed for three weeks after I left," Doar would recall.

John McNally had a football team to worry about, besides watching out for himself. Upon arrival at training camp, young Doar walked past Blood's dorm room where he and assistant coach Walt Kiesling were discussing the next practice session. Blood saw him pass and he caught up with Doar. "Listen, I'm not your shepherd," he admonished. "Don't get any bad habits around here." Doar remembered that the words were delivered "in a humorous way." But he got the picture.

Looking back, Doar reflected on why he wanted to go. "People found it curious that we became good friends," he said. But, in John McNally, John Doar saw something that he wanted too—"taking on something that was pretty different, maximizing your talents in a different way." As a Justice Department attorney in the 1960s, Doar would have a tremendous impact on the U.S. civil rights movement and it would be McNally's turn to stand in awe. "He thought I was opening Pandora's box, tilting at windmills," Doar said. "But I think he was awfully proud. Nobody in New Richmond had any understanding of what I was doing, but John did. In that way, he was broader than others."

Doar also remembered seeing the automatic connection between Blood and Byron White. "Both had enormous mental capacity," said Doar, "and they engaged." But even with White in the lineup, the 1938 season was hardly the success John expected it to be. Karcis remained the team's backbone, and Frank Filchock was added to the roster as a passing back. But John's ability to see eye-to-eye with Rooney was sorely tested. He laid most of the blame for this on Rooney's constant betting at the horse track. Rooney would "be rich one day and broke the next," John told Hickok. "And he had to pay White's salary. He'd take the gate receipts to the track, and, when he lost, he'd sell a player to make up for it."

Watching the Pirates roster was something akin to watching the revolving door from a plush chair in a hotel lobby. Forty-three players came and went or came and stayed in the team's roster during the '38 season. Eighteen of those players were rookies.

Team practices were held on Greenlee Field, a baseball field that served as the home of the Pittsburgh Crawfords of the Negro National League. The field was "uneven and full of rocks," John told Hickok. "It was hard to run ten yards at full speed without stumbling or tripping over something. And there was no hot water, so we had to take cold showers after practice."

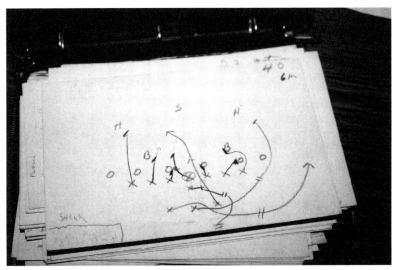

Coach John McNally's Pirate playbook is stored at the Green Bay Packers Hall of Fame. Photograph obtained from and used with permission of the Green Bay Packers Hall of Fame.

The Pirates started their season with three straight losses: 16-7 against the Lions, 27-14 against the Giants, and 27-7 against the Eagles. Next came a 17-3 win over the Dodgers in which the *New York Times* cited John for a "beautiful exhibition of blocking" on a TD by Thompson. Better yet, the Pirates next handed a 13-10 loss to the Giants, the eventual champs of the '39 season. Things were looking up, and John's perseverance was paying dividends.

Unfortunately, the team's financial difficulties led Rooney to begin selling off some of the Pirates' best players. Edgar Manske, Karcis, Ed Farrell, Filchock, and Tom Burnette were all sent packing to other teams for cash. Meanwhile, injuries had wiped out three of John's linemen—Mike Basrack, George Kakasic, and Ted Doyle. John was doing battle with a skeleton crew that all the exhortations of "Pirates don't quit" could not shore up.

The next game was a 20-0 loss to Green Bay in which Blood went the full measure as a blocking back. The next week, another injury forced John to move to the unfamiliar fullback position where he put in another sixty minutes in a 7-0 loss to Washington.

Then came the exhibitions that led to the "missed game" story. It was the penultimate game of the '38 season—a 14-7 loss to the Eagles. Like so many Blood stories, reality and fantasy intersect at only certain spots. The story's foot in reality is that Blood did indeed miss that Eagles game on November 20, 1938.

Roughly, the myth part goes like this: The Pirates traveled to the West Coast for a couple of exhibition games, one in Colorado and the next in LA. They returned for their next game, sans Blood, who'd ventured to Chicago to watch a Packers–Bears game. A sportswriter at the game asked him what he was doing there, and he said his team wasn't scheduled for a game that day. Within seconds, the public address announcer broadcast the score of the Pittsburgh game.

John's account of the story (and the facts) ran quite differently. First off, the Packers were playing the Giants at the Polo Grounds. So, it wasn't the Bears, and it wasn't Chicago. John was indeed absent for a game, but he set the blame squarely at Rooney's feet. He had to wire all the money from the team's two games—a total of $20,000—back to Rooney immediately upon receipt. In theory, Rooney would then wire him money for expenses. Blood got the money to Rooney, but Rooney was slow on his end of the bargain and, when he did send money, it wasn't enough.

So John sent the team back under the watchful eye of assistant coach Walt Kiesling who'd been John's teammate with the Eskimos, Pirates, and Packers. To be sure, John probably didn't sit around his hotel room waiting for more money—he went out to visit his California connections. Eventually, more money did arrive and John returned to Pittsburgh. "He [Rooney] probably took it out of the receipts from the game I missed," John told Hickok.

The following week, in a 13-7 loss to the Cleveland Rams, John put in another sixty minutes at his old right halfback spot. The Pirates' season record stood at a resoundingly sad 2–9–0, putting them at the bottom of the Eastern Division standings. Even with White, the NFL's leading rusher, in the lineup, they posted just 79 points while surrendering 169. A week after the loss to the Rams, John turned 35.

He had been persuaded to return for the '38 season with what he understood to be part-ownership of the team. But what about the '39 season? Knowing full well the pros and cons of his partnership with Rooney, but motivated by his partial ownership of the team, John returned to coach the Pirates. He also remained listed as a back on the Pittsburgh roster, marking his fifteenth season of NFL duty—though he would not see any action.

By this time, John was taking his coaching assignment seriously. He moved the team's training camp to Two Rivers, Wisconsin, where he could tune up his troops against the Packers on a decent practice field in the relatively cooler Wisconsin climate. He approached Curly Lambeau with an idea that was actually quite brilliant from a coach's standpoint: The two teams would play a doubleheader in Green Bay, which would give each of them a chance to evaluate their talent. The games would have 10-minute quarters and abbreviated breaks between the periods.

The first contest featured mostly rookies and free agents and ended in a 7-7 tie. In the second game, Lambeau, who was out to rub Blood's nose in it, played his veterans against John's ragtag crew and won, 17-0.

John finally landed Swede Johnston for the '39 season via a trade. Johnston remembered the deal like this:

> There were about six of us released by the Packers. I was one. Buckets Goldenberg was another. [Actually Goldenberg stayed put in a Packer uniform.] They sent us to Pittsburgh. That's where you wound up when you were through, and that's how I got there …
>
> … So I went to Pittsburgh. Several other guys from Green Bay played for Art Rooney there. Walt Kiesling, who had been line coach at Green Bay, was the assistant coach.
>
> We had a nut for a head coach—Johnny Blood. He'd make up plays during a game. I remember one time I carried the ball, and I ran and ran, but there was no place to go, so I just wound up

and threw it. There was no pass called for on that play. At half-time, Johnny said, "That's the way I want everybody to play." He was an odd one. But you couldn't help liking him.

When I first arrived at Pittsburgh, there was a team meeting and Johnny called the roll. He called out, "Johnston?" and I said "Yes." Johnny said, "Yes, nothing. Pirates never quit!" Everybody was supposed to answer the roll call with that little speech: "Pirates never quit!" He thought he could keep the team all fired up by doing that, but it didn't pan out.

The 1939 season opened against the Brooklyn Dodgers at Ebbets Field, where the Pirates lost, 12-7. The next two contests were also losses—10-0 to the Cardinals, who had finished in the basement of the Western Division in 1938, and 32-0 to the Bears. After the humiliation by Chicago, John presented Rooney with his letter of resignation. His record as an NFL coach stood at 6–19–0.

Walt Kiesling closed out the season as the Pirates' coach and would actually experience some success, and impressive longevity, with the organization. He'd dance back and forth between head and assistant coach as well as on and off the Pittsburgh coaching roster all the way through the 1956 season. In 1940, Rooney would hold a contest to rename the Pirates and, perhaps, bury a bit of their ignominy. "Steelers" would win, an entry submitted by the ticket man's girlfriend.

For Johnny Blood, it was time to catch a train back to New Richmond and collect his thoughts as a thirty-six-year-old man from the comforts of his boyhood bedroom in the McNally home.

John spent the next several months putting a perspective on his NFL career. He'd put in fifteen years as a player and player-coach. By the time he'd put his focus solely on the coaching aspect of the game in 1939, football had been a part of his life for nearly two decades. Now he was faced with something as serious as a death or a divorce. He was a smart enough guy to know what was missing, but exactly what was he to do about it?

From his window in his boyhood home, he could spend some time watching the sun set over Immaculate Conception Church. His room had plenty of books and magazines to read. His walls were covered with maps of the world. But the room also housed all of the trophies and awards he'd won on the gridiron. Of course, the Shamrock Bar was just a couple of blocks away. Kellaher's was a short hike up Main Street. And if he wanted to go for a drive, he could always follow the setting sun to the River's Edge near Somerset. Maybe he'd head out there to reconnect with some old friends. His buddy, John Raleigh, was likely tending bar.

John's presence at the bars was a cause for celebration. Fans around New Richmond who'd watched his football career unfold, thanks to the updates in the *News*, could check the veracity of the many Johnny Blood tales with John in person over a glass of scotch. If they knew how to grease the skids, they'd buy his favorite—Cutty Sark. Eventually, John would find himself spending way too much time with a freshly filled glass of whiskey in front of him. It was filling some kind of void and creating another.

In the fall of 1940, some friends persuaded John to check into the Winnebago State Mental Hospital to "get dried out." He checked in, he said, "with a portable typewriter and a supply of paper," and he left with *Spend Yourself Rich* in hand. His book, he told Ralph Hickok, had been "written in a madhouse." He described the premise of *Spend Yourself Rich* this way: "Poor Richard preached thrift. A penny saved is a penny earned. I set out to show that a penny saved is a penny wasted. As a matter of fact, I wanted to show that it was his thrift that made Poor Richard poor." It was another exercise in John divining the middle of a paradox, this time from a place reserved for such pursuits.

Although he never finished or published *Spend Yourself Rich*, it was one more example of the all-encompassing passion of John McNally's quest for knowledge. In this 150-page manuscript, John explored Malthusian economic theory. Thomas Malthus, who lived between 1766 and 1834, theorized that every individual must have a certain amount of food to survive; with the sex drive as man's strongest passion, it was only a matter of time before the species overpopulated itself into starvation. It was the kind of thing that piqued John's sullen moods.

The thesis in *Spend Yourself Rich* is a curious but bold one—the kind you might expect from a self-proclaimed philosopher delving into economics. It is borne out of John's basic disrespect for economists in the first place, which he shared with Hickok:

I've learned that economics is a quagmire. No one has the full picture. Not Karl Marx or Adam Smith or John Galbraith or Walter Heller—they all have a partial grasp of the subject.

They have more than I have, in the academic sense. But they're just wrestling with serpents. The trouble with the subject is that half of it is inside us and half of it is outside us. A lot of economic reality is based on people's needs and desires and values and distinctions. And we know what a wilderness psychology and psychiatry are.

Classical economics, of course, is based on the idea of the 'rational actor,' and what he will do under certain circumstances. This makes it all theorectical, because finding a genuinely rational actor in real life is virtually impossible. People buy or sell or save or spend because of their hopes, their fears, their dreams, their ideals, their beliefs, what they think they know … In the marketplace, all of the actors are at least partly irrational.

When an economic crisis occurs, the economists are like the expert psychiatric witnesses in a murder trial, testifying vehemently on opposite sides. We don't have this when we send a rocket to the moon. We know when it's going to go, how long it's going to take, when it's going to get there, and where it's going to land. If something goes wrong, we can find out what it was. Economics isn't even close to being science. We've learned the mechanics of production in this country, but we haven't learned the mechanics of consumption.

With chapters like "Money is Not to be Saved," "The Dilemma of Saving," and "With Alice in Wonderland," *Spend Yourself Rich* was not destined to be a textbook in an Introduction to Economics course. John's conclusion was nearly utopian and probably enough to run a roomful of economists amuck:

All of our problems have the same answer: When people get enough courage to consume, they provide themselves with work that enables them to produce and consume more. It is because we are millions of persons that we do not see this.

In other words, since we labor in order to consume, the thriftier we are, the less incentive we have to produce. It is easy to see grandiosity here, a glorification of the economics of the vagrant who works long enough to buy a hot meal or a bottle of wine and then moves on. Where others might see fecklessness, John McNally saw courage.

That he left the state mental hospital with the lion's share of *Spend Yourself Rich* under his arm indicates the extent of his personal transformation. John had departed from the world of football, at least for the time being, but the world of economics beckoned.

Back in Green Bay, the Packers had cruised through three seasons since John's departure at the end of the 1936 campaign. With the awesome presence of Don Hutson in their lineup and Arnie Herber to chuck him the ball, the Packers had finished just behind the Bears in the West in 1937 and gone to the championship game against the Giants in 1938, only to lose, 23-17. In 1939, they'd reclaimed their laurels, slaying the Giants, 27-0, and adding another title to Lambeau's coaching pedigree. It appeared that 1940 would be yet another championship year.

Lambeau began the season with his usual paradigm—fine-tuning his roster through a combination of the draft, resigning his key veterans, and scooping up other people's quality castoffs. Green Bay fans were discussing the team's chances for landing a sixth championship under Lambeau.

By the end of the summer, football fans in New Richmond had reason to take note. The *St. Paul Dispatch* ran a piece titled "'Johnny Blood' Is Galloping Bravely Up Come-Back Road." It had a 38-year-old Johnny Blood working out daily with the Packers and expecting to play in Chicago a few days later against the College All-Stars. "Blood stories," the article said, "are legion in [Green Bay] which has had a hundred football heroes in its years of big league competition, but which still remembers Johnny as the greatest of them all."

From there, the article spun off into a world of inaccuracy; but after all, hype *was* the world of Johnny Blood, and as Art Rooney had said, a story could always be made better. The article relayed the following "incident" in its giddiness over John's return to football. There was, it said:

> [A] time in Chicago when Johnny was missing until shortly before an all-important Bear game. He arrived in time to play— and drew a $100 fine.

Johnny hadn't slept in 2 nights, but he played nearly 60 minutes—knocking down 8 Bear passes and catching 2 that beat them.

The next day the coach lifted the fine.

Then, it told of the New York ice incident replete with John ordering ice water, deciding room service was too slow, and catching a cab to retrieve the block of ice. As an additional embellishment, this version related that the cab driver "followed him with another as they marched thru the lobby to his room." Best of all, next came the Johnny Blood–Father Flanagan story, in which John was "missing on a Thanksgiving day when the team played in Philadelphia. After a frantic search he was found in a restaurant, buying turkey dinners for several poorly clad youngsters."

It was great stuff. Then came the harsh reality, reported in the *News* a week later. Johnny Blood had been ruled ineligible for the College All-Stars game because he had only been signed to play in that one contest. "Officials held," continued the article, "that signing a player for one game only probably would lead to unfair practices in future games." Long-time family friends W. T. Doar and Tom Doar, Jr., had traveled to Chicago to witness Blood's return. "Johnny Blood," ended the piece, "went back to Green Bay with the team."

The following week, Lambeau would again list Blood in his lineup, this time in an exhibition contest against the Kenosha Cardinals of the American Football League. The Packers won, 17-0. A week later, John signed with those same Cardinals for service as a player and assistant manager. In that capacity, John would add one or two more tales to the saga.

The Kenosha outfit was a pretty good one. It lost only two games the whole season, including the one against the Packers. "After the season," John told Hickok, "I still felt like coaching a little more and I read that Winnipeg had won the Canadian championship that year, so I challenged their team to two games, one up there under Canadian rules, one in Kenosha under American rules. We won both games, so I claim the Canadian championship for 1940."

Because Canadian teams used 12 players, John inserted himself into the Cardinals lineup as the extra man. He called it the "lonesome coach" formation in which he'd "go out to the flank to occupy one of their defensive backs. . . . Now and then, for a change of pace, I'd block him."

John also coached the Cardinals for the 1941 season, losing exhibition contests to the NFL's Packers, Giants, Bears, and Rams, but beating their Chicago namesakes.

"I missed a game that year, too," he told Hickok. "But this time it was deliberate." The Packers were playing the Steelers, and though John recalled the game being in Milwaukee, it was actually played in Pittsburgh. Either way, "I went down there for a reunion with some of my old teammates from both teams," he recalled.

That game was played on Sunday, November 23, four days before John turned thirty-eight. His life as well as the life of the United States, was about to be altered dramatically. On Sunday, December 7, the Japanese bombed Pearl Harbor. The next day, the U.S. was an official participant in World War II. John had returned home to New Richmond for the Thanksgiving holiday and his birthday. On December 8, he enlisted in the Army Air Corps.

Another New Richmond lad, Lyle Kellaher, remembered traveling with John as the two of them pulled out of New Richmond by train, headed to their training base in California. Kellaher was a much younger man, though he remembered John being in "great shape" physically. He remembered "wondering why John was enlisting. He didn't have to." Lyle thought it might be one more Johnny Blood adventure, this time on a real battlefield.

But something funny happened on his way to the war. John took a chapter from his Johnny Blood football days and decided riding inside the train was for mere mortals. He climbed on top of the train and crept forward toward the coal tender where he lay on his back, checking out the stars. He told Hickok:

> It was New Years Day, and cold as hell—down around zero, I imagine. But it was also remarkably clear and peaceful. Here I was, headed for a world war, on a train going 60 or 70 miles an hour across country, gazing up at the stars. Everything around me was moving, but the stars weren't. Not that I could notice, anyway. It was reassuring to know that something was eternal.

Johnny Blood, Army private, climbed back into his railroad car the following morning. There was no Lavvie Dilweg to be found, just some upset c.o.s who "were too glad to see me to do anything." John got some license from their forgiveness and, once in California, he decided to visit his friend, Shanty Malone, "for old time's sake." Of course, the visit also ended up involving a girl and—just as he'd almost missed the Packers train to Hawaii in 1932—John decided to push his luck away from the Army (to the tune of nine days of unauthorized furlough).

"I was not alone," he told Hickok. "Quite a few soldiers took the opportunity to have one last fling ashore before getting into the war. However, I certainly was the last one to get on the ship." In California, John trained as a cryptographer. Breaking codes might have bore some similarity to breaking rules or breaking norms and he took to it with some enthusiasm. Eventually his code breaking would take him to Burma, China, and India. As a born seeker, John's time in the Southeast Asian Theater gave him additional perspective. He also had his economic theories, developed in *Spend Yourself Rich*, to apply to the countries in which he served.

All told, John's time in the Army was actually pretty tame compared with his whirlwind tour through the National Football League. He said that his "major contribution to the war effort was teaching Chinese soldiers how to play basketball."

However, that didn't prevent speculation in the States over John's personal war efforts from running a little bit wild. In a piece on Thursday, March 16, 1944, Arthur Daley described a visit from Curly Lambeau. Lambeau had received a letter from the vagabond halfback who was said to be "in India with the ground crew of a bombing squadron." In the letter, Blood wrote that his "immediate ambition is to learn how to operate a bomber and go for a ride some day." According to Lambeau, it all made sense. After all, he told Daley, Johnny Blood had once told him, "I want a sensational life and a sensational finish."

It wasn't John's only letter home. Another went like this:

India
Aug. 11, 1943

DEAR STONEY:
Aloha and all that.

I came 23,000 miles to get here (that's just a little more than what Hutson gains each football season) and zig-zagged all the way like McAfee in a broken field.

We crossed the equator twice, were 60 days on the water (wagon) and then spent a month traveling in what looked like the Toonerville trolley across India. There's always been a lot of hobo in me, but for your information it was all used up by the time we reached the base.

I don't know whether to learn Tibetan, Chinese, Burmese, or Indian [sic]. Guess it will be Burmese and then come home and teach it to the Packers so the Bears can't steal signals.

Toward the end of John's military stint, he gathered honors back in Green Bay as a member of the 25th Anniversary All-Time Packer Team. Named by fans in 1944, John was joined by Lavvie Dilweg, Cal Hubbard, Cub Buck, Buckets Goldenberg, Charley Brock, Mike Michalske, Don Hutson, Arnie Herber, Clarke Hinkle, and Verne Lewellen. A the end of the '44 season, the Packers would land their sixth NFL title.

Johnny Blood joined the Army when World War II broke out, and spent his service years breaking codes in India, Burma, and China. Photograph obtained from and used with permission of John Doar.

On September 2, 1945, aboard the battleship *Missouri* in Tokyo Bay, the Japanese surrendered. John returned to the States a staff sergeant, hung out in California for a short time, and then caught a train back to his touchstone, New Richmond. Days later, he caught a couple of more trains—one on the Soo line and the other on the Chicago & North Western line—so he could return to his other touchstone, Packers training camp.

Once there, Lambeau offered him a position as a part-time assistant coach responsible for scouting the College All-Stars, who were on the docket thanks to Green Bay's winning a sixth NFL championship in 1944. One of John's fellow assistants was his dear friend, Walt Kiesling, on sabbatical from the Steelers.

The proximity to football action tweaked a kinesthetic nerve in John. He asked Lambeau if he might not try his hand on the old gridiron. In an exhibition game against the Eagles, Johnny Blood made his triumphant return for a couple of plays in the second quarter. In the next stanza, Lambeau sent the immortal—though now 42-year-old—Johnny Blood in to return a punt.

"I got under the ball all right, and I caught it all right," he said. "But then, well, I don't know how many Eagles hit me, or what they hit me with, but I don't remember anything else. That was the genuine end of my pro football career." The legendary football saga of one Johnny Blood was ended. In a sense, a train had hit John head on. It was the inevitable train of reality.

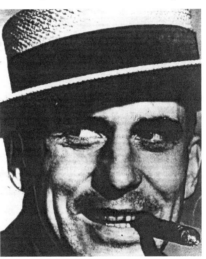

The late 1940s represented some of John McNally's "lost years." He told author Ralph Hickok that he spent some of the time "investigating the effects of alcohol." Photograph obtained from and used with permission of New Richmond Heritage Center.

Chapter 8

Handling the Legend
(1946–1965)

I think I am deeply religious, but I don't believe in any orthodox religion. I mean the problem of the origin of things. It's incredible to me that there could be a world like this and a universe like this. There must be some source beyond what we are able to realize.

— John V. McNally

John's days as Johnny Blood were essentially behind him, or so one would have thought. Leaving the game that had made him famous and that he had made famous wasn't necessarily easy. And in the wake of John's retirement from the pro game would come a bevy of press reports, all trying to paint the picture of just what he had meant to football. In fact, he garnered nearly as much press as a retired football player as he had as an active one. But that made sense because he'd always represented a marriage of amazing feats and legend. Besides, a tame superstar like Don Hutson was never going to drive a reporter's ink the way Johnny Blood had.

On November 27, 1946, he turned forty-three. He'd tried his hand at a myriad of things and had a likelihood of being successful at any one of them into which he threw his entire being. There were those in his hometown of New Richmond who said he could have been a great lawyer—such were his keen wits and analytical skill. There were those who felt he was a natural-born actor—one of the great Blood legends was that he'd outdone

John Barrymore when, in fact, he'd simply silenced a ham actor in a bar. There were those who strongly insisted that had John been given a little more time and a better situation, he could have been a great NFL coach. None of it was meant to be.

No, John McNally had actually found his greatest success as something of another man: Johnny Blood, football artisan extraordinaire. From his position as John McNally, he could dart in and out of his persona nearly as often and as cleanly as he came and went from New Richmond. His greatest success had been on the NFL stage, and now, the curtain had clearly fallen on that set.

In 1946, John gave the New Richmond Roller Mills another try, although it had now changed hands. He became a traveling feed salesman for Doughboy Enterprises. His territory was northeastern Wisconsin, including his adopted home of Green Bay.

"I did fairly well," he told author Ralph Hickok, "not because I'm a good salesman, but because everybody knew who I was, and they'd talk to me about football for awhile, and then they'd buy something. But I got tired of that and quit after a few months."

Early in the 1946 football season, the *Green Bay Press-Gazette* launched a fan poll to name an all-time Packers team. Various Green Bay football experts presented their lists, and fans were encouraged to vote over several weeks' time. When it was all said and done, Johnny Blood and Verne Lewellen were at the halfback spots along with Clarke Hinkle at fullback and Arnie Herber at quarterback. Rounding out the squad were Don Hutson and Lavvie Dilweg at ends, Cal Hubbard and Cub Buck at tackles, Mike Michalske and Buckets Goldenberg at guards, and Charley Brock at center.

One might describe 1947 and 1948 as John's "lost years." He told Hickok that he spent them "investigating the effects of alcohol," though he had certainly examined those effects previously. Perhaps the difference was that this time, he was exploring them as John McNally and not as that irrepressible gadfly, Johnny Blood. Now, those effects had a more serious undertone. Out of the necessity of older age and more time to dwell on them, they lasted longer.

It was during this time that John's cousin, Tommy McNally, observed an event that he called "pathetic." It occurred at the airport where John had driven his mother so that she could catch a plane to visit her daughters in Maine. John was 42 years of age at the time. "I saw John hold out his hand," recalled Tommy, "and from her pocketbook and into his hand his mother placed several bills. She was giving him money." Tommy kept this story to himself, but he said, "It was one of the saddest things I've ever seen."

Eventually, John and Jim took up residence in Kenosha for part of this time, far from the clucking tongues of mother New Richmond. He told Hickok, "This was when I saved my brother's life by making him go cold turkey for a month. But it didn't sober me up. It did slow me down, however. I had the problem that many ex-athletes have: Football had been my calling, and that was gone. I didn't know what to do now. So I drank."

The whiskey may have sucked John to the bottom of the bottle, but he had something most alcoholics don't have: a willing reserve to try something completely unimaginable and unexpected. It was as much a result of jumping from the bridge that July 4th when he didn't want to as it was throwing the pigskin back to a shocked Red Dunn when that seemed the least likely thing to do. So he went to Guam.

"I wanted to go to the Pacific," he said, "but not to a beautiful tropical paradise kind of place like Tahiti—it would have been too hard to think in a place like that. Guam just sort of came to mind, so that's where I went."

John took some books with him, including "the only three books I ever stole." Two of the books, *The Logic of Modern Physics* and *The Logic of Modern Controversy*, John had taken from the Stanford University library. The third, *The Meaning of Meaning*, was purloined from the Milwaukee library. They were nearly perfect books for a man struggling with reality and its meaning. He also hauled along a lot of paper, he told Hickok, "with the idea that I might write something." He never did. He couldn't, because it was a time for questions, not answers. He paraphrased Descartes who said something like, "Once in your life, put everything in doubt."

He also had a copy of *Moby Dick*. John had had a fascination with Melville since he was a young, precocious boy growing up in New Richmond, reading about the whale and his pursuer in his room in that grand McNally home at the junction of Second and Montana. He told Hickok:

> I believe that whale could think. He could read your mind.
> Captain Ahab, a hero of mine, did not realize this. He thought of

the white whale as simple malevolence, unguided by intelligence. And, because he didn't see the intelligence hidden there, Ahab had the courage of ignorance, comparable, I should say, to the courage of a fullback playing his first season of professional football. He hurls himself against the line without being concerned about the consequences.

But go back and look at him at the age of 30. He will not be hitting the line with quite the same abandon. For the courage of ignorance, he has substituted the restraint, the caution, of a little wisdom. Maybe that was part of what I decided in Guam—that I'd spent enough time kind of barging through life with ignorant courage, that it was time to exercise a little restraint, slow down a little.

Late in the summer of 1948, John returned home to New Richmond. For most students, school was just a few weeks in the offing. For John McNally, it was time to set a different course on a new train—this time not by hopping into an open freight car, but rather by taking a seat with something like a ticket in his hand. He enrolled at St. John's University, where he'd left some unfinished business a quarter century earlier. By the end of the spring semester, he'd earned his bachelor's degree and was eyeing a master's degree in economics from the University of Minnesota–St. Paul.

Then, things took a Johnny Blood turn toward the unpredictable. First, he married Marguerite Streater. "Peggy" worked as a secretary at St. John's. Johnny Blood, lover of all women, had obviously left the face of the earth. Like that, the man who'd thrown a pass when he was told to run the ball or lose his job had ad-libbed himself into wedlock. The marriage would last for seven years. Peggy would utter this succinct slogan in describing her man: "Even when Johnny does the expected, he does it in an unexpected way." Peggy saw John put on his cleats and play football just one time during their marriage—in a pickup game with some students and staff on the St. John's campus. But based on that she suggested that, on the gridiron "he always seemed to enjoy himself."

In addition to his sudden marriage, another turn of events would set John McNally on an even steadier course—for a time, at least. St. John's had never done well at football. For all the high hopes that greeted season after season at the small school outside St. Cloud, Minnesota, the realities were nearly always disappointing. As *Scoreboard: A History of Athletics at Saint John's University* said of one football season's forecast, it "appeared promising (they all do!)."

Under coach Joe Benda, the school experienced its greatest success in the early 1930s, culminating in a trio of conference championships. Benda, who'd played under Knute Rockne in 1926 and 1927, was also the St. John's basketball coach. But suffering from Hodgkin's disease, Benda resigned from the hardwood in 1948 and continued through the 1949 season solely as football coach. Green Bay attorney C. J. "Joe" Stodola was a student at St. John's that year and remembered Benda coaching a game against St. Thomas that fall while seated in his car. He was too sick to walk.

In 1950, John McNally took over as head football coach at St. John's University. McNally had begun as a professor of economics and freshmen football coach the year before. Photograph obtained from and used with permission of St. John's University.

Then, in June of 1950, Benda died at the age of 45. He was so revered at the school that he was buried in the Collegeville Parish Cemetery overlooking Lake Sagatagan near the St. John's campus.

The obvious choice to replace him was brand new graduate John V. McNally, who had coached the St. John's freshman football squad to an undefeated season the year before. Coincidentally, he'd also joined the St. John's faculty as a professor of economics for the 1949–1950 school year. He would teach "econ" to the undergrads while he worked on his own advanced degree.

Now there were stories about a previous life of Professor McNally's—about a character named Johnny Blood who'd tripped the light fantastic as a Jazz Age pro football player. But those were only rumors having little to do with the graying academician expounding Malthusian principles in a St. John's classroom, right? Stodola remembered McNally's entrance into the classroom at St. John's on the first day of economics class. He was "in good shape and had graying hair," said Stodola. A classmate leaned over to him and said, "Do you know who that is?" Stodola replied, "Sure, that's Professor McNally." "No," whispered his classmate, "That guy's Johnny Blood."

"John McNally taught me the economic theory of John Maynard Keynes," Stodola said. Keynes, who had died in 1946, had some of the qualities that John McNally valued himself, though they had sometimes eluded him. Keynes had taught at Cambridge University, made a fortune trading in international currencies, and succeeded in virtually every venture he ever undertook. He was also a member of the Bloomsbury Group, a cadre of English intellectuals who exercised great influence in the arts.

Professor McNally, said Stodola, "was a very straightforward teacher, but he certainly made it interesting. I remember the day he walked in and wrote on the board 'What is the business of banks?' and after some students had come up with some fairly predictable answers, he wrote 'They rent money.'" However, said Stodola, "It was pretty obvious that he was not a part of the academic circle of that school."

Stodola described McNally's habit of "coming in a little bit late." It was, no doubt, a touch of John's dramatic persona. So, too, was the early spring that Professor McNally carried a wedge or a putting iron around campus. Sporadically, he'd stop, check his grip, set his feet, and take a swing. It seemed that McNally was planning to traverse the links come warmer weather. "And when it warmed up," said Stodola, "he put the thing away."

"He would have been a brilliant lawyer," Stodola said. "He just absorbed things."

John donned a Packer uniform for one last time on Thanksgiving Day, Thursday, November 24, 1949, in a benefit game to help the team take a chip out of a $90,000 debt. He was joined by Charlie Brock, Lavvie Dilweg, Jug Earp, Tiny Engebretsen, Arnie Herber, Don Hutson, Joe Laws, Verne Lewellen, and Herb Nichols. They did battle as the Girard "Blues" coached by Jug Girard. Their opponents, coached by player Stan Heath, were the 1949 Packers themselves.

Nearly 18,000 fans turned out in the cold and the snow to see the "Blues" defeat the "Golds," 34-31. The field was frozen and slippery, but the Packers' Lumberjack Band still managed to crank out the strains of "In the Good Old Summertime." At halftime, several of the past players gathered for a photo on the snow-speckled field. For the occasion, Lambeau who was seriously under the gun as Packer head coach, donned a helmet and joined the crew of his former players. By January, Lambeau would be through as the Packer coach. He'd been the only coach the team had known since it joined the NFL back in 1921. Packer player Tony Canadeo told author David Zimmerman that the game was far more about raising money than putting your best football stuff on the field.

That's the only game we played where nobody hit the ground! We faked the hell out of that game. It wasn't even as rough as a

John McNally always had a soft spot in his heart for anything Green Bay or Green Bay Packer-related. He returned in 1949 as one of the stars of yesteryear to help the team raise money. (l-r, back row) Tiny Engebretsen, Herb Nichols, Curly Lambeau, Jug Earp, Lavvie Dilweg, Verne Lewellen, and Johnny Blood. (l-r, front row) Charley Brock, Don Hutson, Arnie Herber, and Joe Laws. Photograph obtained from and used with permission of David Zimmerman.

touch game or tag game. You got 'tackled' if someone looked at you sideways. But the fans really came out. I'm proud that we raised a lot of money from the game!

All told, John had a great time reuniting with some of his former teammates back in Green Bay. But he had a more permanent and pressing gig back at St. John's. Through the remainder of the 1949-1950 school year, he gave students at St. John's his take on the world of economics. For its part, instead of dwelling on the capriciousness of the Blood stories, the school embraced the steadiness of John McNally's NFL statistics and churned full-steam ahead into the 1950 football season.

Coach McNally knew the fundamentals of the game, but his freethinking Catholicism was also bound to clash with the Benedictines who ran the school. Photograph obtained from and used with permission of St. John's University.

It was a split decision. St. John's had nearly tied for the conference lead in 1949 with St. Thomas and Gustavus—a one-point loss to St. Thomas had squelched the possibility. But most of the 1949 squad was returning for the '50 season and some of Coach McNally's 1949 freshmen were being added to the varsity. Unfortunately, the team ended up with a 3–3–0 conference record and a fifth-place standing. As fate would have it, the star player, George Marsnick, was banged up for most of the season.

The 1951 season was more of the same, though several new prospects made the light burn a little brighter. One of these was a speedy halfback named Tom White, who naturally had acquired the nickname "Whizzer." Injuries again played a role, and the Johnnies ended their season with 4–1–0 conference mark, good for only fourth place.

Surely, 1952 would be different, wouldn't it? Well, not if the straight-shooting man at the helm of the football ship was to be believed. The August 22 edition of *The Record* had Coach McNally saying, "Things look grim. We expect to have a good line, but we do not know what the back-field will be like." It wasn't exactly the kind of cheerleading that the school expected from the coach.

Fifteen lettermen turned out for signal practice in August with co-captains Bill Christopherson and Maurice Chevalier leading the crew. "But despite the pass-snatching of Jeb Vachuska, the chugging ground-gaining of Casey Vilandre, and the consistent gains through the line by Clem Schoenn-bauer," recorded the *Scoreboard*, "St. John's again ended up with a monoto-nous 3–3 record in the conference and fourth place (5–3) overall." At McNally's expense, the feeling on campus was reported by *Scoreboard* to be "*Il faut que ca change*"—something must change!

On January 23, 1953, *The Record* led with the story, "Coach John McNally Retires; Resignation Effective June 1." The piece had it that John was considering several business opportunities, including some "in his home town of New Richmond, Wisconsin." Above the article was a picture of John signing his resignation papers.

That autumn, John McNally was replaced by a man who would become a coaching legend. John Gagliardi, over the next four decades, became the winningest coach in college football history, leading the Johnnies to more than 400 victories.

McNally's pronouncement upon hanging up his coach's whistle that "Nobody could ever win at St. John's" was still floating in the air as Gagliardi took to the practice field that August. According to many St. John's sources, McNally advised his successor not to take the job, predicting that the

Benedictines wouldn't pay him a decent salary. According to Gagliardi himself, that wasn't too far from the truth. He is reported to have said more than once that "the Friars took a vow of poverty, and they think I did, too." But Gagliardi brought some magic with him; in his first season as coach, St. John's won the MIAC title.

Despite his unparalleled success, Gagliardi understood that old college coaches tend to fade into oblivion, whatever their record may be. "It won't be long before they don't know who I am," Gagliardi told ESPN writer Jim Caple a few years back. "We had Johnny Blood here, and he's enshrined in the Football Hall of Fame. And I don't think there's a single student on campus who knows who he is. Well, maybe one. Eventually, they all forget you. It's not like you're Abraham Lincoln or anything."

"People talk about the pressures of coaching at a big college," John told Ralph Hickok,

> but there are also pressures, of a different kind, in coaching at a school like St. John's.… The monks, and the parents, and even some of the students, give you advice, suggest plays.… And there's so much school pride involved.… I mean those guys in the black suits, the Benedictines, who've been there forever, they say, "We should win all our games, because we've got the best boys, so they must be the best football players, so we should have the best football team," and you say, "What makes you think we've got the best boys?" and they say, as if you're crazy, "Because they're at St. John's." It's hard to argue with that kind of logic, if you call it logic. I didn't even try to argue with it. I got an ulcer, instead.

While a maturing John McNally may have seen himself as "deeply religious," the outward signs, at least to the Benedictines, didn't seem to suggest that. "There was the fact that I didn't go to church," he explained to Hickok, "and the guys in the black suits thought I should. I didn't tell them I'd given that up when I was 17."

Perhaps it was the sudden return of Johnny Blood that closed the book on his St. John's coaching chapter, at least as he told the story to Hickok. He had the team working on a new play during the 1951 season, when one of his players kept missing his assignment. John called the player over and, within earshot of the monks and parents looking on, said, "You'd better make that block next time, or God save your soul—If there is a God and you have a soul."

John was done at St. John's for a second time. Stodola remembered that Professor McNally "just disappeared, never to be heard of again." Or, at least, so he thought.

The following autumn, John found himself in the classroom once again, as what is now called "a returning adult learner." He was working toward a master's degree in economics at the University of Minnesota. It was no big deal for John because he was a learner and because he didn't concern himself with what other people might think of a fifty-year-old student. Besides, he had what one Chicago reporter had once described as "a speaking acquaintanceship with almost every college in the country."

At night, he worked at several odd jobs, which afforded him the time to pour over his philosophy and economics textbooks while on the clock. During the day, he served as an assistant junior-varsity coach for the University of Minnesota under the direction of head coach Wes Fesler.

Much was made of John's connection to Minnesota football by the Twin Cities press. "Johnny 'Blood,' Newest Gopher Coach, Living Legend" read one banner headline in the *Minneapolis Sunday Tribune*. The article had John "going efficiently about his business on Northrop field, giving tips here and there to players who weren't even born before he had already become a living legend." Of course, then the article dipped back into the annals of Johnny Blood lore and dragged out some of the old bromides, adding new flavor as the writer saw fit. Of course, John also gave a nod to his capricious former self, suggesting with a grin that after completing his master's degree, he might "go into politics."

In another piece from the *St. Paul Pioneer Press*, John was quoted on his assessment of promising Gophers quarterback Paul Giel. Giel, claimed McNally, was capable of surpassing the much-ballyhooed Otto Graham of the Cleveland Browns as a T-formation quarterback. "The good T quarters must run in pro football like Graham and Bobby Layne," John said. "Giel would be a wizard coming off the optional run or pass play from the spread in pro football." The *Press* article closed by applauding John's own football days. "Though his fast moving past has carried him to all corners of the globe and to headlines in sports pages across the country," it read, "Blood still says there's nothing like 'that explosion of playing pro football once a week.'" Giel's success wouldn't be quite what John had predicted, though he would play pro baseball for a short time as a pitcher. Still, John's continuing interest in the future of the game in which he'd made his name was noteworthy.

Somewhere in this stretch of time, John and Peggy McNally lived on St. Paul's bustling thoroughfare, University Avenue. In the neighborhood, there were plenty of taverns as well as other places of interest to a retired vagabond halfback and current college student. And while John earned enough credits to claim his degree, he never actually completed the requisite paperwork.

"Without meaning to boast," he told Hickok, "I'd gone beyond what they were teaching me. By that I mean that I had already studied, and rejected, the economic ideas they were trying to pound into me. At 20, or even 30, I might have been interested. But I was getting close to 50 by now, and this was all more of the old snake oil that I couldn't buy anymore."

Joe Stodola would catch wind of Professor McNally at least once more. A St. John's classmate had decided to take a young lady friend into the Twin Cities for a little romancing. It wasn't anything Johnny Blood hadn't done in his day. Stodola's buddy was about to check into a "flea bag hotel under a fake name," said Stodola, "when he looked up at the hotel desk clerk and there was Professor McNally."

John wasn't worried about being found like that, after all he'd come to grips with being noticed a long time before his former student spotted him. But for the aging hotel desk clerk, there was an old aching on which he might not have been able to put his finger. It wasn't long after that, John told Hickok, that he "just decided to cut myself loose and drift again, for awhile." His marriage to Peggy ended. Suddenly, it was 1956 and a 53-year-old John McNally—in the company of a resurfaced Johnny Blood—caught a train back to New Richmond. His old room was waiting for him, and friends and fans back in the City Beautiful were happy to fill John's glass with Cutty Sark.

Then, John's mother died at the McNally home after a long illness, during which she'd slipped in and out of a coma. Mary had passed on to John her thirst for learning, but she'd never intended for it to turn him into a dilettante. "She herself was curious," said John Doar, "but she also wanted something more than football for her son."

John McNally told Hickok of the experience of his mother's death:

> A couple of days before she died, she opened her eyes and looked at me and said, "Well, what will you do now, John?" as if I were a little boy who would be left helpless. And off the top of my head, I said, "I suppose I'll become a prophet."

Mary Murphy McNally was buried next to her husband John in the family plot near the back of the Immaculate Conception Cemetery. John, Sr., had been resting there for some thirty-five years. Eventually, Honor and Jim would join them there.

But in the meantime, John had to become a prophet, of sorts. On the heels of some scotch-soaked barroom bluster, and some arm-twisting and backslapping by three friends, John decided to make a capricious run for St. Croix County Sheriff. And from his campaign for sheriff would emerge one more Johnny Blood legend—although this time, it was really more John McNally's legend.

Someone, it seems, asked John what his campaign platform was and he whimsically answered "honest wrestling." John explained the story to Ralph Hickok this way:

> That was not *my* platform, although that is the myth. I never said that in the county. What happened was I was in Chicago for the College All-Star game, and I went to a party the night before. Somebody asked me what my platform was, and I said, jokingly, "honest wrestling." Well, it got into the newspapers, of course.

John didn't really take his run for sheriff seriously—it was just a reconnect with his former shoot-from-the hip alter ego, Mr. Johnny Blood; a sign that his mature flirtation with "a little restraint" had temporarily ended. He confessed to Hickok that he didn't know what he would have done if he'd been elected. Nearly every story covering his run for sheriff retreaded the old Blood stories, anyway. No one was taking him that seriously. He lost.

For the next eight years, John McNally did as he pleased—the vagabond retired halfback. His mother had left him an annuity that provided him with enough money to continue the life to which he was accustomed: a life in which serious work could still serve as a temporary diversion when desired but was never a demand. Family investments in the thriving Minneapolis–St. Paul communications field were also a dependable source of income. John continued to use his hometown and his boyhood home as his anchor while floating around the carefree lake of life.

VIOLATION	POINTS
Driving under influence of intoxicating liquor, narcotic or dangerous drug	12
Manslaughter or negligent homicide involving use of motor vehicle	12
Felony involving use of motor vehicle	12
Hit and run, involving personal injury or fatality	12
Perjury regarding motor vehicle laws	12
Unlawful use of driver's license	12
Violating occupational license rules	12
Conviction of any violation while license is suspended or revoked, or failure to show proof of financial responsibility when required	12
Reckless driving*	6
Racing on public highway*	6
Hit and run, property damage only	6
Speeding 20 MPH or more over limit	6
Speeding in school zone	6
Illegal passing*	4
Operating without driver's license	4
Driving too fast for conditions, imprudent driving, or failure to have vehicle under control*	4
Arterial or traffic control violation*	3
Driving on wrong side of road*	3
Failing to give proper signal*	3
Failing to yield right of way*	3
Failing to yield right of way to emergency vehicle*	3
Following too closely*	3
Improper brakes or lights*	3
Prohibited or illegal turn*	3
Failing to dim lights	3
One arm driving	3
Speeding up to 20 MPH over limit	3
Illegally driving over sidewalk*	2
Failing to report reportable accident	2
Parking on highway in traffic lane	2
All other moving violations	2
Driving wrong way on one-way street*	1

*If accident involved causes only property damage, add 3. If personal injury is caused by accident due to ANY violation, add 6.

McNALLY FOR SHERIFF

JOHN V. McNALLY
Republican Candidate For

SHERIFF
Of St. Croix County
A Native of St. Croix County
Veteran World War II
Honesty ● Courage ● Ability

In 1958, John McNally made an ill-fated run for sheriff of St. Croix County. It was on something of a whim. When asked at a Chicago party what his platform was, he quipped, "honest wrestling." Photograph obtained from and used with permission of New Richmond Heritage Center.

During this stretch, he would reach sixty-two years of age, and his visage would become far more constant for his friends and family in New Richmond than it had ever been before. It would take some getting used to for everyone involved. John was now more regular in his attendance at local drinking establishments like the Shamrock and Kellaher's in New Richmond, and the River's Edge Supper Club in nearby Somerset.

John Raleigh, his old friend behind the bar at the River's Edge, told reporter Martin Hendricks:

This was one of his watering holes. He was very personable in the bar, a gentleman to everyone, especially the women. Johnny had a photographic memory and could quote Socrates or Plato, verbatim. You don't see that every day in the bar.

Ruth McCabe, owner of the Shamrock Bar, told Hendricks, "My husband, Chris, grew up with Johnny and they were good friends. When he came back to town, he'd always stop in to visit. Folks here appreciated that he remembered his roots."

The depot in New Richmond sits quietly now. But back in Johnny Blood's heyday it was a center of bustling activity. In the background is Kellaher's Bar. Photograph by Rachel Gullickson.

Due to his "St. John's ulcer," Mary Beth Driscoll, McCabe's daughter, remembered seeing John add milk to his glass of scotch. With the eyes of a younger person, Mary Beth observed both the legend and the man. His "brilliance was nearly overwhelming," she said. "He had so much. It took you to some other place. When he walked in, he had such a presence. When he talked, he had such a great face and striking eyes. He was charming. He talked slowly. He had such a great persona."

Of course, Mary Beth also knew his other side. "The whole McNally family had their demons," she said. "There was a certain rage bubbling underneath in John." There were rumors that John had punched a guy in the Shamrock, which Mary Beth confirmed. "But it's certain the guy had it coming," she added. "John wouldn't have hit anyone unless they were really pushing his buttons."

John's alternating time in the Twin Cities made sense to Mary Beth. "He liked the big city," she said. "It had all the things he loved—theater, pro ball. And I think he liked the anonymity of the city. But he sometimes wanted more quiet. He was still rooted in New Richmond."

Lyle Kellaher, who'd been a pretty good amateur athlete himself, would recall John coming into town on the train and getting off at the train depot right across the street from Lyle's bar. Once positioned at the far end of the bar or at the table on the opposite wall, John would start in on his Cutty Sark. He'd also smoke a couple of cigars. After "a few," Lyle said John would sometimes take up a post at the pay phone and start calling people to "give them a piece of his mind about something or another." At those points, Lyle said he felt it was a "drunk Johnny Blood, maybe, making those calls and not John McNally."

Many of those calls, Lyle remembered, were made to Eddie Cashman, who'd married John's cousin and become president of the mill. Cashman had been tagged for the post because, as John's cousin, Tommy, said, "all the McNally men had died by 1932"—meaning John, Sr., and his brothers Fred and Will. John wasn't the only McNally with raised eyebrows, Tommy said, "though John never liked Eddie Cashman." Along with John, others felt Cashman "was not fair to the rest of the family." Cashman had his own problems with alcohol and, at one point, fired Jim, who'd been serving as mill superintendent. In the long run, said Tommy, Cashman "ran the mill into the ground."

At Kellaher's, John McNally was a celebrity, but Lyle remembered that, even in a crowd of appreciative fans, he would often "seem like he was all by himself." Lyle's son, Lee, remembered John "sitting in a booth, reciting poetry." Lyle didn't remember John performing often, however.

Kellaher remembered driving John to the McNally house "more than once." He remembered one particular night when John refused to acknowledge that Lyle had brought him to the right house.

"This isn't my house," John slurred.

"Yes it is, John," Lyle assured him.

"No, it's not. It's another block up," John insisted.

So Lyle drove him around the block back to the same house. There he helped him up the porch to the front door.

Esther Wentz remembered driving on County Road A outside of New Richmond with her husband, Gerald, when they saw John walking on the side of the road. They stopped. "He didn't look very good," Esther remembered. "He'd been drinking. He was disheveled and didn't seem to know where he was. He kept saying he 'was trying to get to J. R. Ranch,' and he had no idea of how to get there." The Wentzs took John home and got him to bed.

When it came to negotiating the familiar stairs in the McNally house, Esther said John more often "crawled than stumbled."

On Thursday, June 16, 1960, *The Minneapolis Star* listed the results of the Suburban Courts. The following entry appeared in the Roseville listings: John V. McNally, 56, New Richmond, Wis., drunken driving, $100.

Despite John's many faux pas, most of them the result of drinking too much, he was almost universally liked in New Richmond—the combination of a great presence and a great legend. From New Richmond, John would travel wherever his wanderlust took him. He would try Hollywood on a whim, then San Francisco. He'd head for Florida for some warmth and sunshine while Wisconsin turned brittle under one more arctic blast.

In 1956, John applied his public-speaking skills and popularity among Packers fans to the effort to construct a new stadium on Green Bay's West Side. Some people were saying that without a new facility, Green Bay, the smallest member city in the NFL, might just lose its team. Many in the league wanted the team moved to a larger city and a bigger market, and Milwaukee and Minneapolis would have welcomed the franchise. A few days before an April 3 referendum on the stadium initiative, John joined Curly Lambeau and George Halas in front of a crowd of nearly 1,000 people at the downtown Columbus Building. "Minneapolis is ready, willing, and able to take over the Packer franchise," John told the audience. "Minneapolis is just finishing a new stadium."

In a piece in the August 28, 1958, *St. Paul Dispatch*, John commented on the present state of pro football:

> It's a faster game than it used to be. That's because of the increased number of players. They get much better pay, the squads are larger, and the size of the ball has been cut down, aiding the

passers. We were lucky in those days to have a passer who could really throw the ball. Now every team has two or three good passers. But players now are seldom used more than 30 minutes in a game. We used to play 50 or 60 minutes.

In the 1960 Wisconsin presidential primary, John crossed paths with a young politician from Massachusetts, John F. Kennedy, who was 14 years John's junior. The Kennedy clan was a strong proponent of the game of football, and John Kennedy had put in time as a sub at Choate and Harvard. Still, the Irish connection was strong. "Your name," he told John when the two met in Green Bay, "was a household name in our home."

He continued to love football, traveling to professional and college games when he could. He especially enjoyed attending NFL championship games. He also visited his old football cronies wherever he could find them—Curly Lambeau, Ernie Nevers, and Don Hutson in California; Whizzer White in Colorado; Cal Hubbard in Boston; and Ole Haugsrud, Bronko Nagurski, and Mike Michalske scattered across the Midwest. During that time, John campaigned actively with his former teammates and others to establish a retirement fund for former players.

During this time, John also speculated about the possibilities for professional football in the Minneapolis-St. Paul area. He predicted that with construction of a 50,000-seat stadium, "pro football will follow major league baseball to the Twin Cities." In 1961, the Minnesota Vikings sprang up as an NFL expansion team (sharing Metropolitan Stadium in Bloomington with the Twins of major league baseball), allaying the fears of a Packers move in that direction. John was known as a frequent spectator at their games, and Mary Beth was sure that he had Vikings' season tickets at one point or another.

In retrospect, sportswriters were slowly beginning to separate John's many solid contributions to the sports world from the Blood persona. Still, nostalgia for Johnny Blood drove most of the headlines. While John became a *cause celebre* for Packers historians like Jack Rudolph and Bud Lea, no one celebrated John's football exploits and his playful whimsy more than Daley in his *New York Times* column "Sports of *The Times*." Nearly every author of the time mentioned Blood's run for county sheriff as his latest feat of whimsy, tying it to the many myths from his playing days. Rudolph wrote that Blood "still retains that indefinable quality called, for lack of a better term, color." Lea said that Blood's "exploits off the field shared the spotlight with his game performances."

John was especially proud and interested in the Packers' resurgence under newly hired coach Vince Lombardi. He would make the trip to Green Bay for Packers home games and spend a couple of days in town, renewing old friendships.

Official recognition of his talent would be forthcoming. And, once it was, it would be practically nonstop. In 1951, John was inducted into the Helm Foundation's Pro Football Hall of Fame, but that was just a start. To commemorate the honor, John and forty other former Packers were introduced at the December 2 game against the New York Yankees and presented with blankets.

On November 16, 1961, John's name was placed in the Wisconsin Athletic Hall of Fame. His former teammate, Don Hutson, was given credit for helping "usher Blood into the state's most exclusive circle of sports heroes."

"'Johnny Blood,'" reported the News, "Puts New Richmond 'On the Map' in State Hall of Fame." John's hometown newspaper reported that "many of 'Blood's' old friends and fans from all walks of life" would attend the awards dinner. "There has never been a more colorful athlete in the history of the state," one New Richmond supporter said. "This enshrinement means another chapter in history."

At the awards dinner, John told a reporter, "It makes more sense to play professional football today than when we played. It was formerly a game for men who just loved the game. Now it's a real stepping stone to a career."

In his introductory speech, Hutson stated:

> Johnny would be an asset to any team on the field today, not only as an offensive player but as one with a winning spirit, which would rub off on a team. Johnny played for fun. And when I think about present-day salaries, I might say we all played for fun in those days.

John's admission into the state Hall of Fame had been sponsored by Doughboy Industries mill, where he'd become something of a regular visitor, working there on and off for many years. In sponsoring John's induction, Doughboy became the first Wisconsin firm outside the Milwaukee area to sponsor a Hall of Fame inductee.

A photo taken at the time showed him with Doughboy vice president Ray Wentzel and long-time employee Albin Asplund. Slung over both of John's shoulders were heavy feed sacks from the mill. This story (and the feed sacks) had been retrieved from John's days working on and off in the mill in the 1940s and 1950s. In order to stay in shape or show off, John had taken to slinging the sacks onto his shoulders and running up the stairs to the mill's second floor. His co-workers were impressed. But not so impressed that they didn't improvise a little prank. They decided to throw a few weights into the sacks and see how John did on his next trip up the stairs. They stood back in anticipation as John hoisted the sacks up onto his shoulders and headed up the stairs one more time. Lyle Kellaher said he later learned that John could tell the difference but "wasn't going to give the other guys the satisfaction of saying anything."

In 1962, John stood by Byron "Whizzer" White's side as he was sworn in as an associate justice of the U.S. Supreme Court—one Rhodes Scholar and one guy who could have qualified but never completed the process. When he'd drafted White for the Pirates in 1937, John had realized that his potential went beyond football.

John's accolades would continue to grow. On September 7, 1963, John was bestowed with an honor by the NFL that only sixteen other men on the planet would share: he was named one of the charter members of the Pro Football Hall of Fame in Canton, Ohio. It was a glorious occasion. Inducted along with John were Sammy Baugh, Bert Bell, Joe Carr, Earl (Dutch) Clark, Harold (Red) Grange, George Halas, Mel Hein, Wilbur (Pete) Henry, Robert (Cal) Hubbard, Don Hutson, Earl (Curly) Lambeau, Tim Mara, George Preston Marshall, Bronko Nagurski, Ernie Nevers, and Jim Thorpe.

John's piece in the Canton repository's special Football Hall of Fame dedication edition read, in part,

> Johnny Blood McNally, a man noted for doing the expected in an unexpected way, played pro football 22 years, 15 in the National Football League.…
>
> He was a wild, colorful character always causing a stir. He broke training rules and ignored curfews.
>
> He was elusive on and off the field. His carefree habits did

not show on the football field too often though. He was all-league several times and held every pass-catching record in the loop until Don Hutson joined the Packers.…

Justice Byron R. "Whizzer" White introduced John:

John has devoted a good many years of his life to the game of football, including 15 wonderful years in the National Football League. Not only was John a magnificent player and a brilliant entertainer, but he had the rarest of all qualities, namely, giving his greatest performances when the greatest was required. This, of course, is the hallmark, historically, of the great athlete and it is also one of the major tests which time applies to the deeds of men. John, you and your performances have survived the test of time, and they will continue to do so.

In his acceptance speech, John said, "You must wonder to yourself, how did I get here? The first thought that occurs to me is that you have to have great luck.… I had that kind of luck and I am very thankful for it." But John also realized that, as a football player and persona, he had had some other help. And so he thanked sportswriters Grantland Rice, Arthur Daley, Arch Ward, and Oliver Kuechle for their "creative imagination and

Johnny Blood became one of the first seventeen men inducted into the Pro Football Hall of Fame. The other inductees included some of his closest friends, who he'd acquired both as a teammate and as an opponent. All agreed that John was one of the sport's earliest heroes. Photograph obtained from and used with permission of John Doar.

magnanimity." He acknowledged their skills in describing plays and events that brought him fame "even I wasn't quite sure had happened." He understood that much of the successful marketing of his Blood persona had come from these writers and their well-worn typewriters.

Over the period, John McNally and New Richmond gained an even greater understanding and appreciation for one another. The city seemed to come to grips with the relationship between their own John McNally and the vagabond persona still celebrated regularly in the nation's newspapers. Midnight trains and open freight cars weren't factoring into the McNally–Blood story quite as much as they had in the old days. John had settled down some. He was learning to handle the legend of Johnny Blood—to meld it back together with John McNally. Still, he was open for a little adventure when it came his way.

It was about this time that one of McNally's students from St. John's crossed paths with him once more. "I was at Louie Van Miller's Standard station in Green Bay," recalled attorney Joe Stodola. "I looked over and recognized Professor McNally. He was pumping gas into an old rust bucket. I mean, this thing had bald tires and everything." So Stodola walked over and introduced himself. "He half-pretended to remember me," Stodola said. "And then I asked him what he was up to and he said, 'I'm headed for California.'" Stodola said goodbye and walked back toward his own car, wondering whether McNally could possibly intend to cross half a continent in the car he was driving.

John may have been behind the wheel of a rust bucket, and the folks back in New Richmond might have still wondered whether John could make it down the road, but in the national press he was still a knight in shining armor. A *Sports Illustrated* feature by Gerald Holland began:

> McNally is tall and lean. He has a strong face and untroubled eyes and a good head of iron-gray hair. He looks like a scholar or a poet or a contemplative monk in mufti. In repose, he is a picture of utter relations and, moving about, he suggests the effortless coordination of a cat. Ordinarily, he speaks quietly and brightly, as though words were not things to be wasted. On occasion, he is not so frugal with them.

Holland recounted many of the Blood stories, suggesting that no matter how wild and unpredictable the legends were, "there was a weird thread of logic running through them." At one meeting, at New York's Dinty Moore Restaurant, John recounted some of his California excursions to connect with Shanty Malone, who he described as a "working philosopher." He suggested that he and Malone had often "discussed some of the great eternal questions."

John also touched on the subject of gambling in football, which had scandalized the game the previous year. John said, "Well, that can't be tolerated today. Frankly, in the old days, we all bet on the games. But we bet on ourselves to win. I never heard of a player betting against his own team."

At that point, John took a look at his watch and told Holland he had to be leaving. He was "on a tour, inspecting lighthouses from Florida to the Canadian border. I am very much interested in lighthouses. My favorite is at Cape Hatteras."

"How did you become interested in lighthouses?" Holland asked.

"I used to go with a lighthouse keeper's daughter," John said as he walked out the door.

John and a number of other New Richmond citizens traveled to the 1964 World's Fair in New York. One day had been dubbed "Wisconsin Day," and Governor Warren Knowles was being recognized as a part of the celebration. Tommy McNally recalled that he and Knowles' wife, Dorothy, rode out to the fair in limousines. Meanwhile, John McNally had disappeared and hooked up with a "blonde babe named Nora who was mad about John," said Tommy.

At one point during a lull in the festivities, Tommy and Dorothy decided to take in the sights. As they neared the Shafer Pavilion, they encountered pandemonium. An ambulance was parked outside. A woman was frantically shouting, "My husband! My husband!" It was Nora. On the floor was John McNally, who had fallen off his chair, drunk. Of course, Nora's hysteria was understandable but why she was screaming that John was her husband was anyone's guess.

Tommy and Dorothy made a hasty departure. Later that evening, the governor joined them, said Tommy, "at a tavern on Third Avenue on the East Side." As they entered, they could see a crowd had gathered around some impromptu entertainer. It was John McNally. "He'd rallied in a big way," Tommy said.

About the same time, John had his picture taken with Burleigh Grimes, who'd been inducted into the Baseball Hall of Fame that year. It was a snapshot that would join, for all time, two of the best athletes ever produced in the New Richmond area—both inductees in their respective sports' halls of fame. John had often been cited for putting New Richmond on the map thanks to his athletic feats.

On Monday night, October 26, 1964, John was the guest of honor at a gathering of 200 folks at the River's Edge Supper Club. The people of New Richmond wanted to show their prodigal son just what they thought of him. In his report of the affair for the *Minneapolis Tribune*, Bill Hengen suggested that John had acquired a new nickname, "The Magnificent Screwball," and that the evening was filled with anecdotes of John's antics. Hengen hung one more tag on John, referring to him as New Richmond's "NFL leprechaun."

John's cousin, Miles McNally, served as toastmaster, telling the crowd, "Blood has many fine qualities . . . though most are deeply hidden." John's old fight manager, Ernie Fliegel, had also turned out and told those assembled of John's short but amazing fight career.

For his part, John told the audience, "the reports of my life have been somewhat exaggerated." He also shared with them a nearly out-of-body experience he'd had once when riding the train through the small town of Roundup, Montana. "There was a hanging going on. I said to myself, 'there but for the grace of God, swing I.'"

John was handed a plaque, honoring him for his football career and for bringing such notoriety to his hometown. He told the crowd he "never felt so honored in his life." The honor seemed to strike a familiar chord in John—the same one that had sounded the day he presented his father with the loving cup he'd won for first place at St. John's field day in the spring of 1921.

As a football elder statesman, John was now often asked his opinion of the game and the players of the day. On Tuesday night, December 8, 1964, John joined retired NFL referee Halsey Hall and former Eskimos teammate Dan Williams as speakers at a Rotary Club Dinner in St. Paul.

John predicted that the American Football and National Football Leagues would soon "get together on drafting players because they'll have to. After all, it is possible to ruin this game, and that would be a shame, because it's a great game."

John then stated that the two leagues "should play the championship game in mid-December, either in Los Angeles or Miami. With television as it is today, there's no need to play in a frozen park in the north. It's not football when you play it on ice." What he was calling for was the merger of the two leagues, which did happen, and a Super Bowl-like championship, which also happened. He was taking advantage of his legend to lend his keen mind and ingenuity to the maturation of the game.

Certainly the Johnny Blood stories were now just history, though John was not above reinvigorating them when invited to do so. Some reporter caught up with John following his Pro Football Hall of Fame induction and asked him what the "famous football phantom" was doing with his free time. The reporter said that John's response came "with twinkling eye and tinkling glass."

"I spend my time doing something that has been neglected for 300 years since Plymouth Rock," John told him. "I wander and meditate. You'll note I said 'wander,' not 'wonder.'"

To Gerald Holland, John explained how he could afford his current lifestyle. "I have a competence from a trust fund."

When Holland asked, "What would you give as your occupation?" John replied, "Reading, studying, writing. Meditating. Once meditation was an honorable occupation. Today, it would appear on a police blotter as a form of vagrancy, I suppose."

On June 1, 1965, Curly Lambeau died of sudden heart attack while mowing a friend's grass in Sturgeon Bay, Wisconsin. He was sixty-seven years old. He and John had last crossed paths on April 26, when John was honored along with Mike Michalske, Don Hutson, Lambeau, Cal Hubbard, and Clarke Hinkle as Packer inductees into the Pro Football Hall of Fame. They had been guests at the Green Bay Elks Club Banquet following Hinkle's 1964 induction.

Upon Lambeau's death, John McNally was contacted in New Richmond and asked to serve as a pall bearer. He would join Don Hutson,

Dick Weisberger, Arnie Herber, Buckets Goldenberg, Charley Brock, and George Strickler. All except Strickler had played for Lambeau. It had poured rain all day and dozens of onlookers watched the pall bearers load the casket into the hearse for the trip down Webster Avenue to the Allouez Cemetery. At the gravesite, the dark, dreary weather seemed to enclose those in attendance like a pall. Mary Jane Van Duyse, who was Lambeau's girlfriend at the time of his death despite being half his age, told author David Zimmerman that she was very self-conscious. "Everybody was looking at me. I was feeling so sad. But the one man that came out with me was Johnny Blood. He loved Curly so much."

Lambeau hadn't conquered the world after all.

Curly Lambeau had worn out his welcome in Green Bay by 1950. By 1965, he was dead. Photograph obtained from and used with permission of the Green Bay Packers Hall of Fame.

Chapter 9

The Legend Meets His Match
(1966–1985)

I may seem lazy, but I care
For my dear ease. My morris chair
Shall hold me snug and warm and tight
While howls the wind out in the night.
While howls the wind out in the day
I'll light my pipe and pull away
In sweet luxurious rolling ease.
While others walk the bounds or freeze —
While they trudge round the frosty bounds
The depths of comfort I shall sound.

— John V. McNally

The wire services spread the story across the nation:

> Altar Beckons Johnny Blood
>
> LAS VEGAS, NEV.—Wedding bells were to ring Tuesday for former Green Bay Packer star John McNally Blood and Miss Catherine Kopp of St. Paul, who is a native of Chippewa Falls.
>
> Friends of the couple said they would be married here by Justice David Zenoff of the Nevada Supreme Court, a former Milwaukee attorney and also a Chippewa Falls native.
>
> Assistant John Doar, a native of New Richmond, Wis., like

Blood, and a long-time friend of the football star of the 1920s and 1930s, said Miss Kopp operates two private employment agencies in St. Paul and one in Minneapolis.

Johnny Blood was getting married. He'd been married once before, to Marguerite Streater, but it had remained off most people's radar, coinciding as it did with his general disappearance from the spotlight while he earned his degree and coached at St. John's. But this second marriage enjoyed no such anonymity, coinciding as it did with John's settling down and his general recognition as a historical figure. It was a clear punctuation mark at the end of a sentence. Catherine was an heiress of the Leinenkugel Brewing Company in Chippewa Falls, Wisconsin. Her mother had been a Leinenkugel.

Was Johnny Blood dead; supplanted, as it were, by a now-mature 63-year-old John McNally with graying temples and a need to find some secure place in the world?

He shared the story of how he met Catherine with his friend, John Doar:

> I went to call on her mother. Well, she was about 40 and I was about 35. But a cousin of mine told me that this woman has a brewery down there and she's very hospitable, drop in. 1935. Catherine opened the door. She was 17 at the time. She said her mother wasn't in town and I said I'm free for the evening, how about you? So we had a couple of dates, I never did date her mother. But there were some people that didn't want me courting their daughters.
>
> In the meantime she married and had 3 boys. She read this article that you have in the magazine, and she dropped me a note saying that she had 3 boys and remembered me and saw this article and that was all that there was to it. A month or so later I ran into her in the City, not by accident, of course, so we were married a couple years after that.

The three boys referred to—Joseph, Michael, and John—became his stepsons and he was known to love them dearly. "They were all adults," Doar said. "But he regarded them as family. He had great respect for all of them. One of the boys was a Marine in Vietnam, and John was extremely proud of him."

After the wedding, John and Catherine took up a rather low-key residence in St. Paul where they would live from 1966 through 1978. Their later years in the state capital would be spent in a modern apartment building at 2028 Grand Avenue, just one block off of St. Paul's prestigious Summit Avenue. It was a quaint residential neighborhood, just southeast of the St. Thomas campus. In many ways, it would be the quietest stretch of time in John's life, something like settling down to watch the sun set.

With her brewing company background, Catherine had some business sense. She opened Kay McNally Placement Services, Inc. An employment agency in a growing, college town was no wild-eyed, scatter-brained venture. John Doar remembered that, while John

John and Catherine. "She knew his history," said Mary Beth Driscoll, "but she appreciated John for his charm and his intelligence." Photograph obtained from and used with permission of John Doar.

was never involved in the day-to-day operations of the agency, he was "very proud of Catherine." By the early 1970s, Catherine was operating two locations—one on University Avenue in St. Paul and the other in the Pioneer Building in Minneapolis.

Mary Beth Driscoll described Catherine as "pretty, affable, a perfect match for John." She added, "Catherine was a wonderful influence on him. She came to his rescue." Catherine was by no means a football groupie, either. "She knew his history," said Mary Beth, "but she appreciated John for his charm and his intelligence." Better yet, Catherine embraced New Richmond, and New Richmond welcomed her warmly. Perhaps its citizens saw her as John's saving grace. "She was a presence, just like he was," Mary Beth said. "She came along just at the right time."

With Catherine's blessing and New Richmond just a short drive from St. Paul, John remained a frequent visitor to his hometown. And the folks back in New Richmond seemed to take a strong liking to this "new" John.

Since John was not tied directly to the employment agency's day-to-day operations, he was able to focus his time and talents on pet projects. He continued lobbying on behalf of retired NFL players like himself, who had given the game their all in the early days but were left without a pension in their later years. John was considered an eloquent spokesperson for this group.

John loved the Green Bay Packers, especially as they regained respectability under Vince Lombardi. He saw Bart Starr as a tremendously talented "underrated" quarterback. Photograph obtained from and used with permission of John Doar.

In September 1970, John was among the first inductees into the Packers Hall of Fame, joined by former teammates Boob Darling, Lavvie Dilweg, Jug Earp, Cal Hubbard, Verne Lewellen, and Mike Michalske, as well as coach Curly Lambeau.

The 1972 presidential election thrust John into the world of politics once more. It turned out that John was not happy with either major-party candidate—George McGovern, the Democrat, or Richard Nixon, the Republican incumbent. He had his own candidate in mind: someone he'd recruited as a football player some thirty-five years earlier, Byron White. White, of course, was well anchored in his post as a Supreme Court justice and could have nothing to do with a presidential campaign.

John Doar, John's good friend, said that the idea of proposing White as a presidential possibility had come from a discussion involving Doar,

McNally, and a number of other friends. But John was the main motivator and organizer in the effort. Doar was far too busy himself to spearhead such a campaign. A New Richmond native who was eighteen years McNally's junior, Doar was well into a successful law career, which had taken him to Mississippi in 1962 as a young attorney working in the Civil Rights Division of the Justice Department. There, he assisted James Meredith in registering for classes at the University of Mississippi after deadly rioting. Three years later, as assistant attorney general for voting rights in the Justice Department, he pushed through the Voting Rights Act, which President Lyndon Johnson signed into law. In 1974, he would advise the U.S. House of Representatives on the Nixon impeachment. All this from the kid who had worked as ball boy in McNally's 1938 Pittsburgh Pirates training camp.

Thus John McNally became the point man for the effort to draft White at the 1972 Democratic convention. "The Dark Horse is White," was probably John's best campaign jingle. He also suggested it was time to "get the All-American off the bench and into the ballgame." As a student of history, John had identified six "dark horse" candidates for president, five of whom had actually won the office.

John listed White's qualifications for anyone who would listen. "Phi Beta Kappa. All-American football player. Rhodes Scholar. Two Bronze Stars in WWII. Magna cum laude at Yale Law School. Strong on civil rights. One of the youngest men ever appointed to the Supreme Court. And then there's the Kennedy association," John told writer Ralph Hickok. White had, John said, "failed once. Just once. He tried to enlist in the Marines, but they turned him down for color blindness. So he went into the Navy instead. Wouldn't it be nice to have a president who'd be color-blind, for a change?"

John was even brutally honest about White's shortcomings, "spinning" them into strengths. "The only fault I see in Byron would be an asset if he ran for office. He's a poor public speaker—make that an ordinary public speaker—but people are sick of these glib SOBs."

The presidential contest itself had begun to heat up that summer, after a break-in at the Democratic offices in the Watergate Hotel on June 17 appeared to implicate President Richard Nixon. The story was just catching fire when Jim Klobuchar, writing in the *Minneapolis Star and Tribune*, suggested that the burglars might have been "looking for the classified plans of Johnny Blood's Emergency Committee to Save the Democrats by drafting Byron White for president." Klobuchar unveiled a plan to kick off the draft-White effort which started with a two-page ad in the *New Richmond News*, entitled "Mr. Justice White, Reasonable Progressive, Man for the Times." The plan was to reprint 50,000 copies for distribution at the Democratic National Convention that summer. The ad had been written, McNally told Klobuchar, by Gary Potter, "the young editor of a Jesus-type East Coast magazine."

Klobuchar described John as "simply an all-purpose phenomenon, evading easy classification." He told the story of John's Notre Dame motorcycle trip, incorrectly identifying it as "a predawn motorcycle ride with a blonde." He also took some gentle shots at the Democrats, describing them as the party "which, until John intervened, was believed to be beyond all help."

McNally, who had run for sheriff of St. Croix County as a Republican, said of being a Democrat, "It's one of the few things I haven't tried. As an independent I feel perfectly qualified to tell the Democrats what to do. The Lord knows they need some advice." He added, "Incidentally, you should disregard some of those accounts of my exuberant youth. That one about the motorcycle, for instance. It actually happened a little closer to midnight."

The White presidency was not to be. Instead, Nixon trounced McGovern, only to resign in humiliation less than two years later over his part in the cover-up of the Watergate affair.

John then barnstormed the country on behalf of pensions for old-time football players. He proposed a three-game series for the Super Bowl rather than just a single game, the additional games helping fund the pension plan. He called his effort "Operation Bread and Circuses." "The people want circuses," he told Hickok, "and the old-time football players need bread."

In the process, he assembled a group of old-timers from the pre-1959 NFL, tagging them "The Naked Alumni." He called them that, he said, "because they weren't covered." He told Hickok that he had passed a tip along to Bob Oates of the *Los Angeles Times*, suggesting that if Oates was looking for a headline, it could go "Blood Covers Naked Alumni."

In 1978, John suffered a mild stroke. As a result, he spent several days in a Minnesota hospital. Old friend John Doar remembered that John's health "had deteriorated some in this period." Doar visited him in the hospital and found the effects of the stroke had put John "in one of his wild moments." In time, however, John McNally recovered and was able to return to his former self.

The stroke wasn't his only health concern. John had been battling a disease, remembered Doar, for several years. "John knew he had something wrong with him and he'd been checking on that." Ironically, what was ailing John, said Doar, was "some kind of blood disease—possibly leukemia."

Later that year, John had recovered to the point where he could travel to Appleton, Wisconsin, where he was honored at a sports award banquet. There, he saw Packers author John Torinus. Torinus thought John looked pretty good "for a man of his years" and he asked John whether he exercised regularly. "No," replied John. "But I think about it a lot."

By fall, it was clear that John and Catherine had to make a change for John's health. John had always had a fondness for California, and they closed Catherine's employment agencies in order to move to the warm weather of Palm Springs. There, they bought a modest home. John would spend the rest of his life basking in the California sunshine, reading, and giving the world "further review." Out there, he saw Don Hutson, who had retired up the road in Rancho Mirage. Byron White and John Doar also frequently visited John. Doar remembered taking a gondola-like machine into the mountains with John. John was studying the terrain of his new home. He did return to the New Richmond area periodically, as he was now a director of the *Tribune* and its related entities.

In 1982, Ira Berkow of the *New York Times* interviewed John for a story with the headline "Drugs & Football." Recent scandals of drug use in the NFL had rocked professional football. John was disarmingly straightforward. He said he'd popped Benzedrine pills or "uppers" as far back as 1935. He didn't think the pill "had any effect on my play, but it sure did give me a lift." He told Berkow, "in the early days of football, with the light padding and the glove-sized helmet, as they were called, a player needed strong fortification to attain an ethereal frame of mind." John also stated that as a merchant seaman, he'd smoked opium, "something they had been doing in China for hundreds, maybe thousands of years," though he "quit fast because I thought it was too risky for my health."

Inevitably, the interview turned to alcohol, a drug with which John had done more than dabble. "I guess I could drink with any man," he said. "I had the reputation, and sometimes I'd drink the night before a game. I was the manic type." Berkow reported that "Blood quit drinking seven years ago." John said:

> I thought I saw King Arthur's Court, and walked through a
> plate glass window to get there. I decided then either King Arthur
> had to go or I was going. Some people can handle drugs better
> than others. But in the end, no matter how well you handle it, it
> ends up handling you.

In 1983, John attended the twentieth anniversary reunion at the Pro Football Hall of Fame in Canton. While most attendees had respected the coat-and-tie dress code, John made his appearance wearing a T-shirt with the name and logo of the Duluth Eskimos on it. He had grown what he called a "Captain Ahab beard" and had taken to wearing glasses.

On September 8, 1983, John's brother Jim shot himself in bed at the McNally home. He'd been alone in the house since Helen's death in September of 1970. Jim had become the owner of the grand McNally home following her death. In his will, Jim left the house to Donna Erickson, his housekeeper of many years.

Donna's handling of the house and its contents caused the McNally family even more pain. John had always used his old room, the second one from the corner on the west side of the house, to store his football keepsakes. Following John's death, a number of football memorabilia dealers were contacted and invited to have at the collection. What resulted was a wide and random dispersal of many of the tangible items associated with the Johnny Blood legend. John Doar was able to retain ownership of some. Today, you can still make a bid on what is purported to be *the suitcase* of the Vagabond Halfback as well as various other items of questionable authenticity.

Tommy McNally told a poignant story of the last time he, John, and John's youngest sister, Margaret, were in the house where so many McNally family gatherings, childhood dreams, and adventures had occurred. Now, it was reduced to a house for sale, its contents going to the highest bidder.

As they went through some of the drawers, Peggy pulled out a pair of tiny wooden shoes she'd gotten in Europe as a child. "Peggy, put those shoes back in the drawer," said John. "They belong to Donna."

With that, the three of them left the house and walked out. They stopped on the sidewalk and turned around to view that wonderful house once more. "Well," said John, "that's it."

In October of 1984, John received an Alumni Achievement Award from dear old St. John's University along with Roger E. Birk, board chairman of Merrill Lynch, and John Simonett, a Minnesota Supreme Court justice.

On Sunday, November 3, 1985, the *Minneapolis Star and Tribune* ran a feature on Midwest Communications, in which the Doars and the McNallys had a financial interest. Because of tremendous growth in the radio and television markets, which Midwest owned along with the *Star and Tribune*, W.T. "Tom" Doar, Jr., John's brother, was proposing a reorganization that would give shareholders a $1,444-per share onetime payout. The families had held stock in the company since the late 1800s and, at least as of 1984, stock dividends were generating about $18,000 per year for each of its stockholders.

Among them, said the paper, was "John V. McNally (Johnny Blood) an early Green Bay Packer who is a charter member of the Pro Football Hall of Fame, now living in retirement in Palm Springs, Calif." Others listed included: Edwin Cashman, "described by relatives as an unemployed world traveler who has been known to change his itinerary after

Eventually John and Catherine retired to California, where they had many visitors out of the old NFL ranks. Here Byron White, then a U.S. Supreme Court justice, joins them. White had played for Coach John McNally as a Pittsburgh Pirate. Photograph obtained from and used with permission of John Doar.

consulting an astrologer"; Joseph E. Murphy, Jr., "a former Minneapolis banker who now divides his time between consulting, writing books, and climbing mountains in Tibet, China, and other exotic locales"; and George Roy Hill, "a Hollywood director whose credits include *Butch Cassidy and the Sundance Kid*, *The Sting*, and *Little Drummer Girl*."

On Sunday, November 24, John collapsed at home and Catherine had him transported to the hospital. It seemed pretty clear that the end was at hand. Catherine contacted Byron White who sent off the following note:

> Nov. 24, 1985
>
> John old friend,
>
> I wish I could be there to see you again. Our friendship has meant a lot to me. I treasure it, there are so many good memories. Marion sends her love to you. She would like to be there. Goodbye, John, and save a place for me.
>
> Byron

In the early 1980s John began sporting what he called his "Captain Ahab beard." Photograph obtained from and used with permission of John Doar.

John Doar quickly flew out to Palm Springs to see his old friend. "I went into his room, and John opened his eyes. I could see that he was pleased that I was there. He didn't say anything."

On the afternoon of November 28, 1985, John Victor McNally died at Palm Springs Desert Hospital. It was a day after his birthday, and it was Thanksgiving Day—just as it had been eighty-two years earlier, the day of his birth. As was fitting, a football game was being played that day between the Lions and the Jets—one of the NFL's oldest franchises (and one that had found its way into the Johnny Blood annals) and one of its newer clubs.

John's survivors included his wife, Catherine, and stepsons Joseph, Michael, and John. Catherine and John Doar had been with John when he died. The exact cause of death was not released out of respect for the family's wishes.

The news of John's death spread across the country. The stars had temporarily gone out. Sportswriters were faced with the difficult task of putting some kind of fitting punctuation mark at the end of the amazing paragraph that was John's life. They also had the balancing act of heralding John's life while breathing even more life into his alter ego, Johnny Blood. One reporter wrote, "by most accounts, he lived life to the fullest." Another described John as "peripatetic."

Former teammate Don Hutson said, "He was a hard-nosed player, all right." But off the field, Hutson said John was "the most affable guy anybody ever knew. I thought an awful lot of him. He already was an established star in the league when I came in. He was a very recognized threat on our pass offense, and that's what I did. He opened things up as far as the offense was concerned. He was a good runner…fast. That's where he really made his reputation."

In its Friday, November 29, edition, the *Green Bay Press-Gazette* led with the news of John's death. Official Packers historian Lee Remmel reflected back to the game against the Providence Steam Rollers when John and teammate Dave Zuidmulder "had been partying intently." As the game approached, Remmel recalled, "neither was anywhere to be seen." When they did show, "neither was in prime condition." Lambeau put both of them in to receive the opening kickoff. Remmel continued the story from there:

> The ball went to Zuidmulder, who started reeling up the field and then lateraled over to McNally. McNally, who was in no better shape, tossed it back to him and they continued that way, back and forth, up the field for the score. The next day the papers were full of stories about the marvelous razzle-dazzle kickoff-return play the Packers had introduced.

In New Richmond, the *News* ran a series of articles on their fallen hero, who reporter Pete Nowacki said, "traveled the world, trying any and every occupation that suited him."

In his second installment, Nowacki spoke with those who knew John best. John Doar said:

> Peripatetic means going here and there, never standing still. That describes him very well. His friends and family never knew what to expect from him. He wouldn't show up at home after season's end, and the next thing you know his mother would get a letter from China, saying that he had signed on as a sailor. John was totally unpredictable, just as free as the wind.

Fritz Friday, whose family was close to McNally, said, "He was a brilliant man. He'd often make his point in a conversation by quoting from literature. He was very well read, a very intelligent man."

A memorial service was held for John in New Richmond on Sunday, July 27, 1986, at Immaculate Conception Church—just a couple of blocks west of the old McNally home. John Doar had organized the service from his law offices in New York. While John's ashes remained in California, a marker was placed in the family plot in the church cemetery. In essence, then, he joined John, Sr., Mary, Honor, and Jim there.

The article describing the service suggested that the event would "put the spirit of the 'vagabond halfback' to rest in the minds of New Richmond residents." For the occasion, Doar assembled a touching memorial booklet that wonderfully commemorated the life that was John McNally's. Doar found it appropriate to include a couple of pieces of John McNally's favorite poetry:

> *I cannot rest from travel: I will drink*
> *Life to the lees: all time I have enjoyed*
> *Greatly, have suffered greatly, both with those*
> *That loved me, and alone.*
>
> —from Tennyson's "Ulysses"

And

> *When he shall die,*
> *Take him and cut him out in little stars,*

And he will make the face of heaven so fine,
That all the world will be in love with night,
And pay no worship to the garish sun.
　　　　　　　—from Shakespeare's *"Romeo and Juliet"*

There are those who suggest that somewhere in the middle of that service, over the prayers and the hymns, a train could be heard churning down the tracks past the New Richmond depot. Some say it was Johnny Blood, the Vagabond Halfback, hopping one more freight train for parts unknown.

An Epitaph

Now that seems very plain and very simple. And it is so. But in the hurly burly of living, it sometimes is easy to forget. Major league baseball managers play "percentage" baseball and so do major football coaches. In the game of life the same rule is at work. Go with the percentage. You may lose but you have a better chance to win than if you go against the percentage.

— John V. McNally

If you're going to write a book on John Victor McNally, Johnny Blood, or some combination of the two, you had better be up to the task. That was the first thing I told myself. And, contrary to McNally's own advice, that doesn't come with playing the percentage. You cannot play it safe and reconcile the disparate parts of his personality and his persona in a manner that is both honest and honoring. How else could you walk down that line of demarcation that so obviously ran through the center of John McNally's life—that sometimes-fuzzy distinction between reality and fantasy, that edge dividing performance from a loss of control, that difference between the light-hearted popular love of the Johnny Blood saga and the darker sense of it by those who knew him best—those two completely separate, yet united, sides of the John McNally/Johnny Blood coin?

John McNally once described himself to author Ralph Hickok as "half stud, half philosopher." He meant that he'd been born under the sign of Sagittarius, the centaur, half horse and half man. Of course, given his legendary sexual prowess, he probably also meant that he had more than once given way to his Bacchanalian inclinations. Certainly he was referring to his many football accomplishments, as well. John's philosophical side was exactly that part of him that prompted the self-analysis.

It was the philosopher Friedrich Nietzsche who suggested that man was made up of exactly those two opposite and, perhaps, equal parts—what he called our Dionysian and Apollonian desires. Dionysus, the god of wine, symbolized the irrational forces in the universe that drive man.

Author Gerald Holland once asked a retired John McNally, "What would you give as your occupation?" John replied, "Reading, studying, writing. Meditating. Once meditation was an honorable occupation. Today, it would appear on a police blotter as a form of vagrancy, I suppose." Photograph obtained from and used with permission of John Doar.

Apollo, the sun god, symbolized the force of order. It was the union of these two forces that Nietzsche saw as a means for propelling man toward a new morality.

John McNally was the type of being that Nietzsche envisioned as a member of the superior race that such a new morality would produce: those free spirits who, unfettered by the normal rules, give the world its greatest beauty, creativity, and energy. "The team lived by one set of rules," John Torinus once wrote of the Green Bay Packers, "and Blood lived by another." And, yet, if Nietzsche's theory holds, these same individuals, wildly different from the masses, often suffer the most.

"John was a scholar, a debater, a thinker, a philosopher," said his friend John Doar. "He had greater intelligence, greater curiosity, greater imagination." But Doar added that John McNally was "something of a disappointment" to his family and friends because:

> John didn't set his focus on anything of value, at least as far as they could see. He was a metaphor for romance. But in a rigid, strict Catholic family, romance isn't a high priority. Balance, loyalty, and devotion to maximizing your talents are.

Of course, the underbelly of romance is despair, and McNally flirted with the darker side of his nature, especially when he was deep in his cups. Perhaps, because he sensed the disappointment of those closest to him. Perhaps, because he sometimes felt a tinge of disappointment in his own inability to negotiate his way along that line. "John had his moods," said Doar. "He was sometimes depressed. Then, John might turn to drinking to wipe that away—to relieve those pressures."

Doar's mother, who was John McNally's first-grade teacher, often said that young McNally "was far and away the smartest kid" she'd ever taught. But she, too, felt the disappointment. "John McNally was not held up at the dinner table in my family as someone to emulate," he said. "My mother was John's teacher," said Doar, "and she loved him. But she also felt he wasted his talents."

It was early in the process of writing this book that Tommy McNally, John's cousin through adoption, told me, "You'd better say in the first paragraph of that book that 'Johnny Blood destroyed John McNally.'" Tommy suggested that the book be called *A Life Wasted* or *Saturday's Hero*. "John McNally played the role of Johnny Blood, rather than living his life," Tommy said. "New Richmond needed a hero, and he was happy to oblige."

Tommy, who'd come to grips with alcohol a long time before, suggested that John had never faced his own demons. He recalled a time in the living room of the McNally house when he and John's brother, Jim, were doing well in Alcoholics Anonymous and John "was on one of his benders."

"John was leaning up against the fireplace," Tommy remembered, "and he said, 'You guys are quitters. You let John Barleycorn beat you.'" Jim and Tommy told him that he should quit, too. But John would hear none of it. "He just kept saying 'You guys are quitters,'" said Tommy. "He could be amusing when he was drunk," Tommy said. "But he could also be mean." No doubt a person with superior intelligence and charm could find himself frustrated with himself and others.

An amusing John was the kind that Tommy recalled on one particular Sunday. The day was gorgeous, and Tommy and a friend were seated in a car outside of the McNally house when down the front steps, "John comes bounding out." He climbed into the backseat and announced, "We're going to take an excursion." So the three of them headed out to Cedar Lake to visit Johnny Roach who had a place there. John had a "few drinks," said Tommy, "and he was really funny that day." On the way back into New Richmond, John began shouting, "Stop! Stop!" They pulled over in front of a schoolhouse where John said, "Behind yonder schoolhouse one sheriff's wife robbed young John Victor McNally of his innocence."

On the subject of drinking, John himself told author Ralph Hickok:

> My parents hardly ever drank. They were naturally high, naturally elated people, and a couple of drinks might have sent them out of sight. I'm the same way, except that I do drink. It's a family thing. I've had three or four cousins die of alcoholism. My brother probably would have, too, but I saved his life—locked him in a hotel room for a month, brought him food, wouldn't let him drink, and it cured him. But I could never cure myself. Alcohol really hangs onto me. It's partly because I don't eat; I'm one of those people, if I take two or three drinks I don't eat. It just

shuts my appetite off. Now that I've thought about it for many years, I think it's probably an unconscious drive just to have the experience that's going to happen to me.

Whether or not Johnny Blood destroyed John McNally is a question that calls from the fine line between fantasy and reality, which John McNally often stumbled along on his scotch-laden walks home from the Shamrock Bar—the chasm in which McNally lost himself on more than one occasion. It was the dichotomy of mind and body, of reality and legend. Doar called it "John's dilemma." It was the tension between McNally, the man, and Blood, the persona—a balancing act that John often failed to pull off. Doar said:

> John was blessed with a terrific, extraordinary talent. He was born with a remarkable body and a remarkable mind. Perhaps that was his dilemma—being caught between a remarkable body and a remarkable mind. Now that I say it that way, it makes sense to me. It was the tension between them and the inability to reconcile the two that explains the depression. He was smart enough to see that, and he couldn't really be both. He never wanted to get the mantel of Johnny Blood off his shoulders. He wasn't apologizing for Johnny Blood ever. Johnny Blood brought joy to John McNally. But he was smart enough to see that he couldn't really be both Johnny Blood and John McNally. That he couldn't have success in both of those lives. He was too restless.

Walking that line, after all, really was (and is) a question of balance. "He may have regretted that he didn't have the balance to maximize his talents," said Doar. "He often commented on my brother, Tom, saying that Tom had balance. Balance and discipline weren't John's strongest characteristics. It was an observation of a quality he admired and wished he had more of himself."

John's legendary drinking and his legendary womanizing were, perhaps, the manifestations of his "dilemma." After all, they were the dashes of salt and pepper that seasoned every great Johnny Blood story. Yet even these two themes are tempered by contradiction.

"He took women by storm," Tommy McNally said.

"I don't know about his affairs," said John Doar. "He wasn't a braggart. Women found him attractive. He was good looking, kind, humorous, thoughtful, clever—I mean he had all the tickets."

Yet this ardent gadfly, this womanizer of the first magnitude, was also said on more than one occasion to have rented out an entire whorehouse for the night—only to spend time with the girls inside, chatting, and reading them poetry.

John's womanizing was as mythical as his drinking. How much self-control was there in either? New Richmond still rings with rumors of an alleged affair between John McNally and Dorothy Knowles, the wife of Wisconsin Governor Warren Knowles. If those rumors are true, then some lines were crossed. On the other hand, it seems just as possible that "affair" was a definition assigned a relationship by others that might not understand a friendship between two attractive adults without sex.

"John and Dorothy Knowles were good friends," said Doar. "They liked each other's company. Did they sleep together? That, I don't know. I sure don't have any proof of it. Do you? John wasn't a braggart that way and, when it came to other people's impressions of something like that, he didn't give it a second thought."

Still, John's dalliances with numerous other women are well documented. If even half the stories of John's wildness are true, then we know he embarrassed himself and others sometimes—especially later in his life as expectations of greater maturity, responsibility, and adherence to social norms increased. While drinking factored into most McNally stories—giving John's sometimes off-the-wall actions some impetus or explanation—there were certainly those who saw the whole thing as an Irish wake taken far too far.

Doar suggested that, especially in John's later years, drinking and womanizing hardly made a smooth blend:

> I don't think when he was drinking he was particularly attractive. I can't speak to those incidents from early in his life. I certainly don't connect that part with his being older and drinking. I never really saw that part of him. But when he was drinking, he was kind of wild. He'd jump from subject to subject and get off on tangents. Some things were hard to follow.

Doar said that an older John McNally openly expressed to him "missing the counsel of his father. I think he regretted not having his father around to guide him more. In fact, I know he did. He told me that. He may have thought, when he looked back, that he may have missed something."

John may have desired more balance for himself, but there were times when he seemed to exhibit a fair share of his own. When he was sober, all agreed that he was at his charming, intelligent best. Eventually, he'd come to grips with his demons and show people what Doar called "a thoughtful, kind, terrifically smart, loyal, special individual." Seven years before his death, John quit drinking. It was a major turning point in his life and yet he did it without fanfare or a public announcement of any kind. Those who knew him well suggest that his marriage to Catherine was a major step toward his salvation.

Some aver that it was John's eternal youthfulness that helped deflect some of the harsh blame he might have been due. "He clung so fiercely to boyhood," one writer put it, "he never grew up"—tapping directly into the Adonis myth. "My parents had tried to make me master the violin and be a debater and recite poems," he said once. "But I had a high resistance."

He skated across the open water of most of his trouble as the irrepressible Johnny Blood, his *joie de vivre* providing enough momentum to do that. Doar said, "Take the story of the Northland Hotel when he first moved to Green Bay. He put wax on the floor and played the music. That kind of joy was appreciated by all people."

The sports world itself remembers Johnny Blood with kindness. Among sportswriters, he had many fans and promoters who found, in him, a model whom they could paint with their greatest words. He was "blithe" to one, "a fleet-footed and free spirit" to another. One called him "hawk-like and handsome" in appearance. But they all seemed to agree on "colorful," "unpredictable," and "talented." Richard Whittingham suggested that after all was said and done, "Johnny Blood was as well-liked by the football players he ran with and continually entertained as he was by the chorus girls he dated and also entertained."

"Most stories about Johnny Blood are fables," Tommy McNally said. "I once asked him about running for a touchdown backward or something like that, and I never did get a straight answer."

And like fables, the stories have taken on lives of their own. And like a good self-promoter, John did little to set those stories straight, letting them spin in various directions instead—sometimes, perhaps, at his own expense. He was also known to tell varying accounts of the same story. Some "Blood stories" have only one foot in truth and the rest of their being in fiction.

John was as popular amongst his former teammates as he was when they played together. Here (l-r) Mike Michalske, Don Hutson, Curly Lambeau, Call Hubbard, Clarke Hinkle and Johnny Blood have gathered at a 1965 Elks Club event to celebrate Hinkle's induction into the Pro Football Hall of Fame. Photograph obtained from and used with permission of David Zimmerman.

Take the story of how John McNally came to be Johnny Blood. All tales agree it involved a theater. But after that, it is an example of Mark Twain's adage, "get the facts first, young man, and then distort them as you wish." Various accounts have John and Ralph Hanson strolling by the theater, cruising by in a car, or driving by on a motorcycle. According to John's cousin, Clarence J. Mulrooney, they were on bicycles. There's the version where they were actually sitting in the theater, and the version in which John simply remembered the name of a Rudolph Valentino movie while lugging stereotypes at the *Tribune*. One reporter even had the theater located in a small Wisconsin town. John Doar himself wasn't sure that the other man involved in the story was Ralph Hanson, believing instead that it was some guy named "Fitzgibbons or something like that." Doar also thought that the theater was in Duluth.

In nailing this event down once and for all for this book, the story began to look something like wily Johnny Blood himself—twisting and turning to escape a would-be tackler named Fact. The most logical route for John and his buddy, Ralph Hanson, to have taken from work at the *Tribune* that day was due south on Nicollet Avenue. After all, the newspaper offices sat on the corner of Second and Nicollet. It was a straight shot of twenty-four blocks to East 26th Street and the Liberties' practice field. But McNally had told Richard Whittingham that the movie house they'd passed with the *Blood and Sand* on it was on *Hennepin*! Not only was Hennepin an illogical route to take, there were nearly a dozen movie houses on Hennepin (and only one on Nicollet)! Suddenly, the story had unraveled.

There was yet another problem. *Blood and Sand* had been released in 1922, not 1924. As Terry Stokke, a Minneapolis researcher said, "We aren't New York City, but there's no way *Blood and Sand* was making its first run in Minneapolis in 1924." We did know that Valentino's 1924 film, *Monsieur Beaucaire*, had found its way to Minneapolis on September 7, 1924, and was showing at the Garrick Theater on 7th Street. So, the story had to be that John had taken Hennepin south, swung east on 7th en route to Nicollet, which they would take to their tryouts on East 26th Street. The only possibility for the story, as told to date, was that Valentino had been identified as "The Star of *Blood and Sand*" on the Garrick marquee advertising *Monsieur Beaucaire*.

But how could one simple story have spun so completely out of control? The answer is simple: John McNally allowed it, and Johnny Blood encouraged it.

Did John actually slit his wrist in order to sign an autograph in his own blood? Or was that just another story with no truthful foundation? (And, perhaps, a story that John himself set in motion or allowed to continue to run until it ran out of gas?) The event was real—having unfolded as the Eskimos raced across the country on their football barnstorming tour. A young woman was involved, and John impressed her by signing an autograph in his own blood. Few things could have been more dashing and indelicate at the same time.

"What did you do that for?" Ernie Nevers asked John after he cut his wrist. "Now you won't be able to play tomorrow!"

"Who said I won't?" John scoffed. The following day, he played his usual sixty minutes.

The Blood mystique was as much a part of the game of football as it was the game of McNally's life. Above all, John understood the art of self-promotion and he did it under an alias, providing himself plenty of cover and plenty of room for slipping back and forth between reverie and actuality.

His former teammates appreciated John both for who he was and who he was not. "Johnny was similar to Don Hutson," said Clarke Hinkle in the Wisconsin Public Television video *The Grandstand Franchise.* "He could do the 100 in under 10 seconds. He had great moves. And it was uncanny how he could get in between a couple of defenders and for some unknown reason come up with that football all the time. As far as the fundamentals of football—the blocking, the tackling—Johnny wasn't too adept at that."

Charley Brock said, "He was a type of football player probably something like Paul Hornung. He was a Sunday football player. He could do a lot of things that other athletes couldn't do on Thursday, Friday, and Saturday and still go out and play a terrific game on Sunday."

Few appreciated Johnny Blood more than Don Hutson, a fact that is rather amazing. After all, they were men on opposite ends of a spectrum. Hutson was quiet and unassuming. His flash came from his lanky frame and his incredible athletic skills, which made his feats seem especially elegant. Johnny Blood, on the other hand, was a showman, whose athletic talents were merely one more prop in his performance, no more or less important than his on-field ad-libbing or infectious grin. At times, that seemed to haunt John. Referring to himself in the third person, he said, "They'd say, 'yeah he can play. He plays the ball all right. But he'll lose you games as well as win 'em.' And so my answer to that was 'well, just name me one game that I lost.' I never found anybody who had an answer to that."

Hutson chuckled when the subject of Johnny Blood was raised. "Due to the length of time I'm going to have on this program," he said, "I don't think I can start on McNally. You should have a serial on him running once a week for an hour."

And through the discussion you can hear the same line being walked. Was Johnny Blood a football player to be evaluated on the rubric of his skills or a show-business persona to be appreciated as an effective-but-whimsical performer?

Even John McNally described his gridiron career in terms different from most aging football men: "I have no complaints about the eighteen years I spent at it. I got my emotional income for it that I wouldn't have gotten any other way or any other time. It just fit my style."

Football fit his style. "Style." That thing the French call *"je ne sais quoi"*—

something difficult to describe or express, something unreal and ethereal.

Still, there is plenty of reality to be had. Blood played for 15 seasons—16, if you count the one night in 1941 he played for the Buffalo Tigers of the American Football League. (In that game, against the New York Americans, he played under his real name, carrying the ball five times. He had taken the night off of his Kenosha Cardinal coaching duties in order to suit up.)

With the Packers, he wore jersey numbers 24, 26, 27, and 55. With the Pirates, he wore number 53. Over his NFL career, he played in 137 games and had 498 running attempts for 1,638 yards or a 3.3-yard-per-carry average. He scored 5 rushing touchdowns. He caught 172 passes (37 of them for touchdowns) for 3,034 yards, a 17.6 yard-per-catch average. He returned 27 punts for 359 yards and a touchdown. He also returned one kickoff for a touchdown. He picked off 35 passes and ran 5 of those in for touchdowns. He completed 58 of 159 passes for 869 yards and 4 touchdowns. He threw17 interceptions. He punted the ball 179 times for a 36.6-yard average. He led the NFL in touchdown pass receptions in 1930 and 1931.

He could, quite literally, do it all. And when he retired, his 37 career touchdown receptions and 224 points were league records. And his fifteen seasons were played not as an offensive or defensive player but as both. It was what he called the "one-platoon system." He was named as one-fourth of an all-pro backfield that included Red Grange, Ernie Nevers, and Dutch Clark. He was named to the first All-NFL team in 1930 and 1931, to the second team in 1929, and to the All-1920s NFL team. He was, of course, a charter member of the Pro Football Hall of Fame.

Of course, it was the "intangibles"—those traits that came from the Johnny Blood legend and fed back into it—that most football historians have noted. Not the least of these was his great on-field presence and his ability to turn the game around as a "clutch hitter." He played the game almost as two wildly different people: One was a clown who would horse around when his team was firmly in the lead, and the other was a fierce competitor capable of spectacular last-second plays when the game was on the line. This split persona only fanned the flames of the Johnny Blood legend.

Don Hutson once summarized the skills he observed in his teammate as follows:

Johnny Blood was one of the last great individualists of the football field when it was still called a gridiron. Like Red Grange, Bo McMillin, and Jimmy Conzelman, he had the speed, the change of pace, the swivel hips, and the quick eyes to break loose on his own and run through the opposition, whereas today's great backs largely depend on perfect execution of well-drilled blackboard plays laid out by their coaches. Johnny Blood could improvise, make up plays on the spot as the occasion demanded. I don't suppose this always made a hit with his coach, but his performance did.

By the height of his NFL career, John had indeed become his hero of the Roman wars, Cincinnatus. Hutson once said this of Blood's presence on the field:

I never saw a fellow who could turn a ballgame around as quickly as Johnny Blood. When he came into a game, the whole attitude of the players changed. He had complete confidence in himself. He had tremendous football sense.

Despite his own superior talents, Hutson observed in Blood something that he felt lay outside his own abilities. Hutson was arguably the greatest receiver to ever play the game. But his talent was constant—never waning or waxing to the point he could single-handedly affect a game he hadn't already affected. In Johnny Blood, he saw a fellow player who could reach down into an infinite well of talent and performance and absolutely change the direction of a game. In the eyes of one of the game's greatest, Hutson, John McNally was the ultimate clutch hitter. So much so that Blood's mere appearance in the Packers huddle could bolster the faith and performance of his teammates.

Nearly every football writer took a whack at capturing John's fleet-footed capers and off-field escapades, as well as his indescribable impact on a game. Some actually nailed it pretty well, and others simply let their purple prose add to the confusion, discarding the veracity of the story in favor of embellishing the fantastic. John's favorite writers were Grantland Rice, Arch Ward, and Oliver Kuechle. Kuechle described Blood this way:

He could be with riff-raff in a waterfront bar one day, then recite Keats or Shakespeare by the hour in different company the next. He could drop a pass thrown right in his hands, then catch one that nobody else could. He could hand over his $100 to an acquaintance in need and pass an overdraft for $5 on a friend (which he invariably made good).

The world is full of people who affect color—who swim the Hellespont with water wings. Not Blood. There was nothing boastful about him or synthetically erudite. He did what he did and said what he said because he was Blood. He argued on things because he really knew them and because he happened to hold strong opinions. He traveled with bums on occasion because he wanted their company. He recited poetry—and he could do this by the hour—because he liked it.

The inevitable question of any football player from the past is "Could he play today?" It's a little like asking whether Ben Franklin, if dropped into the 21st century, could become independently wealthy by as early an age as he did in the 18th century. It is inherently a matter of comparing apples and eggs. Still, as a student of the game, as a player, coach, and fan, John had some thoughts on the subject. "There are a lot of factors involved," he told Ralph Hickok. He continued:

There's no doubt that the players today are bigger—and faster for their size, probably. Most of them are better coached than some of our guys were. Also, if you assume that a certain percentage of the male population has certain skills that make them good football players, the number has obviously increased, simply because the population has increased.

John went on to assess a number of his fellow players, suggesting that guys like Cal Hubbard and Hutson would still make the team today. But he also imagined changes that some of his other former Packers teammates would have to make in order to remain in the huddle. But Hickok pressed him: "What about Johnny Blood? Could he play today?" Finally, John responded:

At the risk of sounding boastful, I have to say I could. Remember, I'm a little unusual, like Cal Hubbard, in that I was big for my position at the time. . . . Of course, those small guys are there because of speed, but I had that, too. I was never clocked in a real dash, but remember Hutson only beat me by half a stride when I was thirty-two years old, and he was a consistent 9.7 in the hundred. . . . Yes, all in all, I think if the Packers had Herber and Hutson and me, and Hubbard and Michalske, and Dilweg, and Lewellen, and Hinkle, all in our primes, right now, we'd have the nucleus of a pretty good pro team.

Over the years, John continually renewed his relationship with the Packers. His attendance at Packers events was dependable right up to the point where his failing health prohibited it. His presence on the Packers sideline was a thing to be celebrated by fans, and he was available anytime Green Bay football needed a spark. When Vince Lombardi took the wheel and righted the ship in 1959, John continued to be a great supporter. He was especially fond of Bart Starr, who he considered an "underrated, highly effective quarterback."

Of course, John's own approach to the game ran a bit more parallel to Golden Boy Paul Hornung's, as suggested by Charley Brock. (Some may even wonder whether Hornung hadn't found Blood's old "How-To" manual lying around in the Packers equipment room—given his own collection of anti-curfew excursions.)

Hornung told reporter Martin Hendricks that he had a picture of himself and John hanging in his office in Louisville, Kentucky. "It's a picture of Johnny Blood and me that was taken up in Wisconsin," Hornung said. "And it's signed, 'Two of a Kind.' I think Johnny outdid me, but then I played under Vince Lombardi."

The night before a home Packers game in 1978, John ran into *Minneapolis Star and Tribune* sportswriter Jim Klobuchar at the Northland Hotel—John's old haunt from his playing days.

"Hello, John," said Klobuchar. "No, I don't want to hear 'The Lay of the Last Minstrel.' I don't want to hear Kipling's 'If,' either. It reminds me of the wasted opportunities of my youth."

"Tonight I have chosen from John Donne," McNally returned. "No man is an island, entire unto itself. Every man is a piece of the continent, a part of the main. If a clod be washed away by the sea, Europe is the less, as well as if a promontory were . . . ."

"Don't you just throb with brotherhood?" John paused and asked Klobuchar before he continued.

Today, John's life and times as a Packer are celebrated in the Packers Hall of Fame and in a dining room named for him at the Lambeau Field Atrium. His name is scattered throughout the Packers record book as a runner, receiver, return man, kicker, and passer. While Green Bay has no street named for the Vagabond Halfback, he's a regular thought at the old Chicago & North Western depot, now Titletown Brewery, where you can order a pint of a delightful Irish red beer that bears his name. On second thought, forget the street sign. Naming the stretch of railroad tracks running alongside the old depot for him would be far more appropriate.

The McNally House is being restored to its original grandeur. Photograph by Rachel Gullickson.

Finally, what of the City Beautiful and its relationship with its Vagabond Halfback today? They still remember Johnny Blood in New Richmond. After some years of neglect and mistaken attempts at modernization, the McNally house is being restored to its original splendor. And John's life is well documented at the Heritage House Museum and the C. A. Friday Memorial Library. His name still brings a few shakes of the head and smiles as "Blood stories" are rehashed at Kellaher's and the Shamrock Bar. The regulars there still remember where John sat and what he drank. They remember his lively banter, as well as his more sullen moments. Even the young people at the bar have heard of Johnny "Blood" McNally and sense his presence.

Dave Newman, sports editor for the *News*, still lends an ear to anyone with a new take on Johnny Blood. In 1998, Newman reminded his fellow citizens of their homeboy. In a full-page piece titled "Johnny (Blood) McNally: Former pro football star was a fun-loving, intellectual hero of his generation," the *News* recounted many of the old anecdotes of its prodigal son.

Newman wanted his readers to know both sides of John McNally. Most were familiar with the spectacular football feats of Johnny Blood; John's place in his hometown's history has pretty much been cemented as "the most famous athlete New Richmond has ever produced." But what "people often do not know about McNally," Newman wrote, "is that along with being a gifted athlete, he was a free-spirited person with a brilliant mind."

As long as fans of football and fans of the human heart and mind exist in New Richmond, the memory of John Victor McNally will be a part of his hometown—the one with which he had such a mercurial relationship all of his life.

Johnny Blood hasn't been forgotten at Lambeau Field. His image greets fans on the steps leading to the Packers Hall of Fame, looking as handsome and unpredictable as ever. Photograph by Denis Gullickson.

Trains still run through New Richmond, though they don't pick up passengers at the depot any more. Cars still head north and south through town on Knowles Avenue, and kids still play in the city parks. On fall evenings, a pickup game of football starts in some kid's backyard—one team pretending to be the Packers and the other the Vikings from over the state line. John McNally might not live here any longer, but Johnny Blood —that free spirit who tells us to warmly embrace everything this world has to offer— always will.

John McNally was given a marker in the family plot at Immaculate Conception Catholic Church although his ashes remained in California—making John about as elusive in death as he was in life. Photograph by Denis Gullickson.

Bibliography

ARTICLES

Henry, Jack. "Johnny Blood: The Vagabond Halfback." *Professional Football Resources Association Web site, www.footballresearch.com/articles/frpage.cfm?topic=blood*

BOOKS, BOOKLETS, AND PAMPHLETS

Blanck, Thomas and Charles Locks. *The New Richmond Walking Tour: A Guide.* New Richmond, WI: The New Richmond Preservation Commission. n.d.

Cope, Myron. *The Game That Was: The Early Days of Pro Football.* NY / Cleveland: World Publishing Company, 1970.

Doar, John. *John V. McNally: November 27, 1903—November 28, 1985.* New Richmond, WI: N.p., n.d.

Falcone, Vincent J. *Great Thinkers, Great Ideas.* Norwalk, CT: Cranbury Publications, 1988.

Goska, Eric. *Packer Legends in Facts.* Germantown, WI: Tech/Data Publications, 1995.

Goska, Eric. *Green Bay Packers: A Measure of Greatness.* Iola, WI: Krause Publications, 2004.

Gullickson, Denis J. and Carl Hanson. *Before They Were the Packers: Green Bay's Town Team Days.* Black Earth, WI: Trails Books, 2004.

Harrington, Denis J. *The Pro Football Hall of Fame: Players, Coaches, Team Owners and League Officials, 1963–1991.* Jefferson, NC: McFarland & Company, Inc., 1991.

Hickok, Ralph. *Vagabond Halfback: The Saga of Johnny Blood McNally.* New Bedford, CT: N.p., 1991.

Johnson, Chuck. *The Green Bay Packers: Pro Football's Pioneer Team.* New York: Thomas Nelson and Sons. 1961.

McAlister, Virginia and Lee McAlister. *A Field Guide to American Houses.* New York: Alfred A. Knopf, 2005.

Names, Larry. *The History of the Green Bay Packers: The Lambeau Years, Part One.* Wautoma, WI: Angel Press of Wisconsin, 1987.

——. *The History of the Green Bay Packers: The Lambeau Years, Part Two.* Wautoma, WI: Angel Press of Wisconsin, 1989.

——. *The History of the Green Bay Packers: The Lambeau Years, Part Three.*

Wautoma, WI: Angel Press of Wisconsin, 1990.

——. *The History of the Green Bay Packers: The Shameful Years.* Wautoma, WI: Angel Press of Wisconsin, 1995.

Peterson, Robert W. *Pigskin: The Early Years of Pro Football.* New York: Oxford University Press, 1997.

Sather, Mary A. *They Built Their City Twice: A History of New Richmond, Wisconsin.* New Richmond, WI: New Richmond Preservation Society, Inc., 1998.

Schlesinger, Arthur M., Jr., gen. ed. *The Almanac of American History.* Greenwich, CT: Brompton Books Corporation, 1993.

Torinus, John. B. *The Packer Legend: An Inside Look.* Neshkoro, WI: Laranmark Press, 1982.

Tucker, Dustin OSB and Martin Shirber OSB. *Scoreboard: A History of Athletics at Saint John's University; Collegeville, Minnesota.* Collegeville, MN: Saint John's University Press, 1979.

Whittingham, Richard. *What a Game They Played.* New York: Harper and Row, 1984.

Woog, Adam. *A Cultural History of the United States.* San Diego: Lucent Books, Inc., 1999.

Zimmerman, David. *Lambeau: The Man Behind the Mystique.* Hales Corners, WI: Eagle Books, 2003.

Zimmerman, David and Stephen Zimmerman. *The Scrapbook History of Green Bay Packer Football.* Hales Corners, WI: Eagle Books, 2005.

_____. *Official 1997 National Football League Record & Fact Book.* Los Angeles: NFL Properties, Inc., 1997.

NEWSPAPERS

Chicago Tribune
Green Bay Gazette
Green Bay News-Chronicle
Green Bay Press-Gazette
Minneapolis Journal
Minneapolis Star
Minneapolis Tribune
Minneapolis Star and Tribune
New Richmond News
New York Times
St. Cloud Daily Times
St. Paul Dispatch
St. Paul Pioneer Press

VIDEOS

The Grandstand Franchise. Produced for Wisconsin Public Radio by Larry Long, University of Wisconsin–Green Bay. 1984.

Index

207